D1563260

To Dad,

With lots of Love,
Christmas 1980

Angie and Roland

MORE TALES OF TENNESSEE

Also by Louise Littleton Davis
Frontier Tales of Tennessee

LOUISE LITTLETON DAVIS
MORE
TALES
OF
TENNESSEE

PELICAN PUBLISHING COMPANY
GRETNA, 1978

Library of Congress Cataloging in Publication Data

Davis, Louise Littleton.
    More tales of Tennessee.

    "Stories that have appeared in the Sunday magazine of
the Tennessean over the years."
        Bibliography- p.
        Includes index.
        CONTENTS: Judgement day on the frontier.—Politics
and pistols on the frontier.—William Blount, first impeachment in the Senate.—He killed Tecumseh.—The white-hot
blaze of courage.—And then there were none. [etc.]
        1.   Tennessee—History—Addresses, essays, lectures. 2.
Tennessee—Biography—Addresses, essays, lectures.   3.
Statesmen—United States—Biography— Addresses, essays,
lectures. 4.   Presidents—United States—Biography—Addresses, essays, lectures. 5. Frontier and pioneer life—Tennessee—Addresses, essays, lectures.   [1. Tennessee—History—Addresses, essays, lectures.   2.   Tennessee—Biography—Addresses, essays, lectures. 3. Frontier and pioneer
life—Tennessee—Addresses, essays, lectures] I. Title.
F436.5 D38   976.8   78-15957
ISBN 0-88289-183-9 lib. bdg.

Manufactured in the United States of America

Published by Pelican Publishing Company, Inc.
630 Burmaster Street, Gretna, Louisiana 70053

Dedicated
To the memory of
Silliman Evans, Sr.,
late publisher of The Tennessean,
whose enthusiasm for Tennessee history
inspired these stories

Preface

Publication of *Frontier Tales of Tennessee* in 1976 came in response to readers who had asked to have in book form some of their favorite stories that have appeared in the *Sunday Magazine* of *The Tennessean* over the years. The final decision on which stories to include came down to which had been most frequently requested.

Since that book appeared, there have been more requests for other stories from *The Tennessean* about the state's early days. In this volume of nineteen more stories, there is a different approach in selecting them. In the first volume, every man ventured forth on one frontier or another—Matthew Fontaine Maury, for instance, in mapping ocean floors; Augustin Gattinger in discovering and cataloguing plant life in Tennessee.

In this second volume, most of the men and women share the harsh adventure of arriving early on the scene in Tennessee and American history. Some of them, like patient John Ross, are Indians who tried to make peace with the white settlers. Some—like William Blount, whose secret deals with the Indians placed him in the unenviable position of being the first member thrown out of the United States Senate; and Richard Mentor Johnson, non-conformist tavern-keeper and protege of Andrew Jackson who was propelled into the vice-presidency because of his fame as killer of the dreaded Tecumseh—are white frontiersmen whose fame rose or fell, depending on how they dealt with the Indians.

For the most part, stories of purely local interest have

been excluded. But it is difficult to limit Andrew Jackson to
any one area, and his influence threads the frontier in count-
less ways. Though only one story focuses on the complex
Jackson, he shows up in other stories that reflect various
sides of his character. Jackson's loyalty to old friends shows
through in the story about Colonel Thomas Butler, proud
veteran of the Revolutionary War who was prepared to defy
the United States Army, the president and the Supreme
Court rather than cut his hair. Jackson's temper flashes
through the story of his smoldering feud with another rugged
frontierman, John Sevier, Tennessee's first governor.

In another mood of adventure and daring, men from
many parts of the nation took their stand to protect their
rights at the Battle of the Alamo in San Antonio, Texas. But
there were more men from Tennessee at the Alamo than
from any other state, and their dashing leadership—whether
sharp-eyed David Crockett holding the weakest portion of
the fortress, or romantic Jim Bowie (inventor of the Bowie
knife) rousing men to new valor when he was too weak to
stand—rings out in shining, icy, endless valor.

In another mood, James K. Polk, first showing his courage in a fight against illness, battled his way methodically,
with cold calculation, to stretch the nation's borders to the
Pacific, from Mexico to Canada. Another Tennessee president, Andrew Johnson, came under the spell of a scholarly
British minister who finally retreated to the mountains of
North Carolina to live as a hermit and ponder the world's
fight for freedom.

There are men with the vision of Richard Henderson,
who "bought" most of Tennessee and Kentucky from the
Indians and cut a wide swath through the dangerous wilderness to plant white settlers here.

In a much later era, in perhaps the saddest and most romantic story of all, there is the young school teacher who
lived the rest of her life as a widow, doing great good for her

community after the man she was engaged to marry was hanged as a Confederate spy. It was, after all, Lincoln who had gone back on his word and allowed the young Confederate soldier, Captain John Yates Beall, to be hanged without a fair trial. The fact that Lincoln met his own death exactly seven weeks after Beall's death has stirred many to put together the misty scraps of evidence that tie the two events. There are those who believe that Beall's hanging triggered John Wilkes Booth to action in his long-planned plot to kill Lincoln.

On another political frontier, in Russia's icy St. Petersburg of almost 130 years ago, another Tennessean, former Governor Neill S. Brown, as minister to Russia, felt "unseen eyes" following him through frozen streets to invade his very room and mail. Russia's ambition even then to overpower the United States was obvious to Brown, and Russia's use of secret agents and petty schemes were chilling shadows of events to come.

Perhaps nowhere in the book does the toughness, the sternness of early Tennessee come home more vividly than in two tales of justice on the gallows and at the whipping post and in the church—frontier style.

Acknowledgements

To Amon Carter Evans, president of *The Tennessean,* and John Seigenthaler, publisher of *The Tennessean,* for permission to publish these stories, all of which appeared originally in *The Sunday Magazine* of *The Tennessean.*

To Harriet Chappell Owsley (Mrs. Frank L. Owsley), former director of the Manuscript Section, Tennessee State Library and Archives, and present co-editor of the Andrew Jackson Papers, for her endless help in directing me to little known sources for many of these articles.

To the entire staff of the Manuscript Section, Tennessee State Library and Archives, for their assistance in my search for much of the material.

To the Library of the Daughters of the Republic of Texas, San Antonio; the Library, University of Texas, Austin; and the Texas State Library, Austin, for much of the material on Tennessee men at the Alamo.

And especially to the readers of *The Tennessean* who have volunteered information from their family records and lore to add to the tales of courage and high adventure in building Tennessee.

Contents

MORE TALES OF TENNESSEE

The Big Land Grab

When Judge Richard Henderson and the arrogant Edmund Fanning "traveled together" to a North Carolina courthouse that September morning in 1770, Nashville was "as good as born."

Some say the first blow for national independence came then. Certainly it spurred Carolinians to the first of several conventions demanding freedom. For Fanning, the most hated man in powerful Orange County, North Carolina, represented the British government in the minds of many of the taxpayers he oppressed, and the mobs that filled the Hillsborough, North Carolina, courthouse that Saturday, September 22, 1770, came armed with whips and clubs. If Judge Henderson, one of the two judges on the state's superior court, didn't hand down justice to Fanning and his crowd, the rough-shirted "Regulators" would show them how.

The black mood of the rock-throwing crowd meant the end of Henderson's career as a judge. It showed him, unmistakably, that the time had come to push the frontier westward. These angry men—the Regulators—were not going to take any more gaff from the overbearing manipulators of Virginia and North Carolina politics.

The whole uprising boiled to a white heat when Fanning, the snobbish county register eight years out of Yale, was caught red-handed: he had consistently overcharged farmers and small businessmen in their taxes and kept the excess.

He had a retinue of officers who helped him, the Regulators charged. One of them was Francis Nash, the man for whom Nashville was named some ten years later. Nash was county clerk, and it was his job to collect the taxes that Fanning assessed. The sheriff was in on the deal, too. When a farmer could not pay his taxes, the sheriff would confiscate horses as payment.

Two years earlier, Fanning and his crowd had faced formal charges of tax abuses in court and had been found guilty—all but Nash. But they had never been sentenced. In blind anger the Regulators seized a horse the sheriff had taken as payment of unjust taxes, "beat up the sheriff, shot up the house of Edmund Fanning," and threatened to come back to town with a force of fifteen hundred men to "burn down the town." The governor had called out the militia and promised the Regulators that their case would get a new hearing. This Saturday morning, September 22, 1770, was the day set for that hearing.

On the way to court that morning, Judge Henderson and Fanning were waylaid by the Regulators and the latter was threatened with instant death. But Judge Henderson persuaded the men to take the matter to court, and, after a short and threatening session that morning, he was able to adjourn until the following Monday.

The fury of the crowd gained momentum during the weekend, and when Judge Henderson entered the courtroom at eleven o'clock Monday morning, he found the Regulators packed in "as close as one man could stand by another." Even as Judge Henderson yielded to some of their demands, the crowd grew restless, and some of them threatened to strike the judge "while he endeavoured from the bench window to moderate their fury." They made a lunge for Edmund Fanning, and when he darted to the bench for protection, they dragged him out by the heels and mauled him with clubs until he wrestled loose and fled to a nearby store. There they broke the windows and pounded him with stones.

Nash escaped in the confusion. The only reason Judge Henderson escaped without a "whipping" was that he promised to hold court until the end of the term. He admitted later that he had no intention of keeping his promise. "At about 10 o'clock that evening I took the opportunity of making my escape by a back way, and left poor Colonel Fanning and the little Borough in a wretched situation," he said.

Wretched indeed was the little borough. All through the night the Regulators patrolled the streets, breaking windows, burning barns, shooting things at random. They helped themselves to the courthouse records and made obscene entries. Then they ran Fanning out of town "as fast as he could go," with dogs at his heels and stones flying. Fanning's house and all his belongings were burned. They also burned Richard Henderson's house, barns, stables, horses, and grain. They terrorized the town.

No court was held until the following year, after the militia defeated the Regulators at the Battle of Alamance. Six Regulators were executed and many others imprisoned. Judge Henderson, thirty-five years old at the time he was chased from the bench, never returned. His fortune had suffered, and he was eager to make another with one of the boldest land ventures in all American history.

Son of a genial sheriff from Virginia, Henderson knew well Daniel Boone, son of a county squire. For years Henderson had dreamed of settling the wildly beautiful Indian territory that young Boone had told him about—the land that stretched west of Virginia into what would one day be Kentucky, and the land that stretched west of North Carolina into what would become Tennessee.

Actually Henderson had paid Boone to scout the territory for him some six years earlier. Boone had told him about the satisfactory agreement James Robertson had made with the Cherokee Indians to get the land for the Watauga Settlement in East Tennessee.

Henderson, an astute lawyer, consulted legal authorities in both England and the colonies. He decided to take the direct approach: he would buy some eighteen million acres—approximately all of Tennessee and Kentucky—from the men who had first claim on them, the Cherokees. He would thus by-pass the claims of Spain, France, England, Virginia, and North Carolina to these lands. Once he had the Indians' agreement on the deal, he would open the biggest real estate business in history.

Henderson had several partners in the business, including his kinsman and law partner, John Williams, and Thomas Hart, a "sturdy, honest, and brave man" who had been sheriff of Orange County and had served in the North Carolina house of commons. The land company was finally organized as Henderson and Company, and its new colony was to be called Transylvania.

Henderson, who had been recommended for his court appointment as "a gentleman of candor and ability, born in Virginia and living in Hillsboro, where he is highly esteemed," had married the daughter of an English peer. He was a charmer, a man of "unusual mental capacity" who had inherited his mother's "strong, very strong talents." Frontiersmen who starved and bled with him in their Kentucky and Tennessee ventures were loyal to him as a man who was "always fair."

Henderson directed the gigantic project of settling Kentucky and Tennessee from the first. He had lively and often vicious competition. George Washington was eager to push his land holdings west, and he looked with suspicion on Henderson's activity in that direction. Thomas Jefferson was said to be eager to be in on Henderson's deal. Patrick Henry was so eager to be a member of the firm that he dickered with Henderson for some time about the terms. But Henry

finally decided that it might not be the wise thing to do polit-
ically. With the Revolutionary War brewing, politics was
especially risky.

Virginia and North Carolina were still British colonies
then, and British officials in the colonies were eager to participate in the land grab. Officials of the crown piously
reported to London all of the activities of Henderson,
because he had beat them to the coveted land. Even in
London, the craze for "western land" had British heads
spinning with dreams of wealth. When wealthy investors got
word that Henderson and Company had made a gigantic land
purchase from the Cherokees, the legal machines began
grinding.

But Henderson, with Boone as his guide and constant advisor, had struck out across the mountains and through the
forests to meet the Indian chiefs himself and set a date for
the big land sale. He and his company invited "The Little
Carpenter," chief of the Cherokees, to come to what is now
Fayetteville, North Carolina, to choose the goods they would
like to have in payment for Tennessee and Kentucky. For
months Henderson's company had been busy hauling wagon
loads of blankets, guns, ammunition, flour, corn, hogs, rum,
salt, ribbons, and wrist bands to be paid the Indians. Henderson said he delivered "10,000 pounds" worth of goods, in
British money. At any rate, the wagon loads were stored at
Sycamore Shoals, near the present Elizabethton, Tennessee,
where the white leaders were to meet Indian chiefs to work
out the deal.

The Indians began arriving at Sycamore Shoals for the big
meeting in January 1775. By February, there were almost
twelve hundred Indians there. "The Little Carpenter," over
ninety years old at the time and weighing not much more
than ninety pounds, was chief of all the Cherokees, the
"wisest man" among them. He had won his name because, as
a diplomat, he, "like as a white carpenter could make every

notch and joint fit in wood, could bring all his views to fill and fit into their places in the political machinery of his nation."

Among the white men at the meeting were Henderson, John Williams, Thomas Hart, Nathaniel Hart, James Robertson, John Sevier, Isaac Shelby—all striking figures in the building of Tennessee.

For twenty days the white men and the Indians negotiated. It was a heart-breaking decision for the Cherokees, but they agreed to sell their lands for the wagon loads of goods, and they agreed not to molest the white men who were coming to settle there.

There were five hundred North Carolina families ready and waiting for the signal to start the rough journey to new opportunity, Henderson said. He hired workmen to cut roads through the wilderness, and he advertised fantastic inducements for settlers. They would protect each other by living in fortified towns, and they could claim vast farmlands nearby. Henderson and Company would pay soldiers to protect the settlers—pay them with five hundred acres of land, that is. Any man who would set up an iron works would get five thousand acres of land free. Any "salt manufacturer" would get five hundred acres of land free, and so would operators of saw mills and "great mills."

On the great day that Judge Henderson led the procession of emigrants out of Hillsborough, North Carolina, the whole populace turned out to bid them good-bye. "They marched out of town with considerable solemnity," one of the townspeople wrote in the spring of 1775, "and to many their destination seemed as remote as if it had been the South Sea Islands."

Daniel Boone had already led one of Henderson's parties into the wilderness, in Kentucky, and they had been attacked by Indians. Boone's own son was one of those killed.

"We are on thorns to fly to Boone's assistance, and join

him in defense of so fine and valuable country," Henderson wrote hurriedly. That same day, in April 1775, Henderson crossed the Cumberland Gap, and there he met forty of Boone's party returning from Kentucky "on account of the late murders by the Indians."

"Could prevail on only one to return," Henderson reported sadly. "Several Virginians who were with us returned home." It was like Columbus sailing into unknown seas; yet Henderson and his men kept pushing ahead until they arrived at Boonesborough, the little settlement that Boone had established in Kentucky. Some idea of their speed comes from an account of their arriving on Tuesday, staking out sites for their new homes that same day, and moving in that same week.

> In the Eavening we git us a plaise at the mouth of the creek & Begin clearing. . . . Wednesday 26th We Begin Building us ahouse & aplaise of Defense to keep the Indians off. . . . Satterday 29th We git our house kivered with Bark & move our things into it at Night and Begin houskeeping.

Practical problems beset Henderson from hour to hour, and one was "to stop the great waste of meat." Some of the settlers, in their wild abandon at the sight of plentiful game, "Would kill three, four, five or ½ dozen buffaloes, and not take half a horse load from them all." As a result, "Our game, as soon as we got here, was driven off very much. . . . Fifteen or 20 miles was as short a distance as good hunters thought of getting meat."

But the great hunger was for bread. In fact, the fastidious Henderson himself wrote of his long hunger. Corn, wheat, grain were not to be had until harvest. "Continue eating meat without bread," he recorded. "No meat but fat bear. . . . Almost starved. . . . Drank a little coffee and trust to luck for dinner. . . . "

Henderson paid Daniel Boone for his services with a two-thousand-acre grant of land, and Boone settled his family at Boonesborough. There Indians bedeviled them, kidnaped their daughters, and made every day a life-and-death gamble.

By 1778, opposition to Henderson's "empire" in Kentucky had gained such strength in the Virginia legislature that they voted to strip him of the land he claimed and repay him for his trouble with a grant of two hundred thousand acres in an inaccessible part of Kentucky. Those two hundred thousand acres were not marketable for twenty years, long after Henderson's death. And the only reminders of his pioneering in Kentucky today are the county and town named for him. The town, beautifully planned around a park bordering the Green River, is near the Ohio River, in the northwest corner of the state.

When Virginia took Kentucky away from him, Henderson put even more energy into developing his Tennessee land. He not only induced James Robertson and John Donelson to make their now famous trips to Nashville by land and by river, he also bought corn in Kentucky to ship by river to the hungry outpost on the Cumberland. Corn is said to have cost two hundred dollars a bushel, in Continental money, in that frozen winter of 1779, when James Robertson and party walked across the Cumberland to "French Lick" (Nashville).

By coincidence, on that same icy Christmas that Robertson and his party arrived at "French Lick," Henderson arrived at Boonesborough to bargain for the corn. But trouble was all about him. He still felt a personal responsibility for the Boonesborough settlers, who were shivering in what one of them described as "the extream cold weather, Together with Nakedness of myself and people . . . and the poverty of my horses. . . . "

Moreover, James Robertson and other settlers thought that the Nashville site would fall within Virginia, rather than North Carolina. Henderson had to be sure it was in North Carolina to have any hope of claiming it. He was traveling with the Virginia surveyors as they crossed the state marking the line between what is now Kentucky and Tennessee.

On Christmas Day, 1779, the surveying party arrived at Boonesborough, and soon after that they set out for French Lick (Nashville). On the way, they met John Donelson and his party, who had been stalked by Indians, death, and disease almost from the beginning of their river journey from Watauga Settlement, in East Tennessee. (They had traveled the length of the Tennessee River, then up the Ohio River and dipped down again to the Cumberland River, toward Nashville.)

It was March 31, near the mouth of the Cumberland, when the two parties met: "At this meeting we were rejoiced," Donelson wrote. "We are now without bread, and are compelled to hunt the buffalo to preserve life. . . . " On April 24, Donelson's party arrived at the Nashville site, where Robertson and his men welcomed them to log cabins they had built "on a cedar bluff above the lick."

Henderson and Hart began building a fort about six miles away from Fort Nashborough, on Stone's River, near Donelson's settlement. There Henderson drew up the complex Cumberland Compact, including organization of the government and rules for settling land claims. He opened his land office and began selling one-thousand-acre tracts for ten dollars each. He was already contending with claims of George Clark, William Byrd of Virginia, and various others for the Nashville land.

In that same spring of 1780, in the midst of the revolutionary war, our colonies began offering vast parcels of Tennessee land as a reward to soldiers who would enlist. Henderson left Nashville to busy himself in North Carolina politics to salvage his land. He was elected to the North Carolina legislature, where, in spite of his efforts, all he could save of his Tennessee venture was reimbursement for his trouble. In May

1783, the North Carolina senate granted Henderson and Company two hundred thousand acres in "Powell's Valley," in East Tennessee, "as compensation for their expenses, Trouble & Risque in settling the lands. . . . "

Two years later, when Henderson was forty-nine years old, he died at his plantation on Nutbush Creek, near Hillsborough, North Carolina. It was many years later before heirs to his company realized any profit from the inaccessible acres that North Carolina had awarded them. Conflicting land claims and lack of ability of the heirs to get the land surveyed delayed the sale for years. When it was finally sold, it went for fifty cents an acre.

Lost—or hoarded—is all of the correspondence and other papers showing the exact agreement between Henderson, the man who financed the settling of Nashville, and James Robertson, the man who scouted the area and helped develop it.

Not even a street or a single monument in Nashville commemorates Henderson, the elegant North Carolina lawyer who staked his fortune and his health in opening up the west—centered in Nashville. Only his old friend Francis Nash, who dashed out of the courthouse with Henderson some fifteen years before—with a mob at their heels—left his name first on Nashborough and then on Nashville. He had to become a hero in the Revolutionary War and be killed at the Battle of Germantown to win the honor.

John Ross
of the Cherokees

The white man, John Ross said, was the tornado.

The exotic, improbable top chief of all the Cherokees warned his fellow tribesmen where the storm would strike next. Already the Choctaws, the Chickasaws, and the Creeks had fallen. In 1834 Ross said the Cherokees stood like a lonely tree in a wasteland, "an open space, where all the forest trees, save one, had been prostrated by a furious tornado."

Four years later, the tornado had blown the Cherokee off his Tennessee-Georgia land forever. The infamous "Trail of Tears," leading seventeen thousand banished Cherokees along a twelve-hundred mile, six-month-long route of winter suffering and death, would end in Oklahoma and more broken promises. Only a remnant, the few who hid high in the Smokies, remained in the East.

Ross, a strange mixture of white and Indian, had seen the tragic end coming for a long time. Only one-eighth Indian himself (on his mother's side), he was haunted by the thought that the Cherokee might disappear altogether.

Solidly educated, well versed in the classics, and as much at ease in Washington drawing rooms as in the forests of the Smokies, Ross threw his fate with the Cherokees. A slender man with light brown hair and high cheek bones, Ross had the Cherokee's unyielding stare. He was a man of medium height, compactly built and meticulous about his dress. His Cherokee name, *Cooweescoowe*, means Large White Bird.

Longer than any other Indian chief in American history— for nearly forty years—he remained "principal chief of the

Cherokees." He wrote their constitution, modeled after ours, and he set up a supreme court for the Cherokees, also patterned after ours.

It was his dream that the Cherokee, most highly civilized of all American Indians, could so blend his way of life with the white man's that they could live peaceably side by side. Ross's heartbreak over that failure spills out in letters and other papers acquired by the manuscript division of the Tennessee State Library and Archives. The state bought them from Mrs. Penelope J. Allen, who got the treasured collection from the chief's grandson.

Ross tells how his people had believed in one American treaty after another, only to see it broken. They had fought for America, only to be cast out as "foreigners." He wrote in 1834:

> There is no security for our permanent residence anywhere else within the United States and the only alternative left us will be to seek homes within the dominion of some other power. Our existence as an independent nation is drawing to a close.

With soldiers' guns at their backs, the Cherokees were pushed out of their Tennessee and Georgia homes to an unknown "West." That was the winter of 1838-1839, when Ross's worst fears came true. His own wife, a Cherokee, died on the "Trail of Tears." Crippled Indians, old and ill; infant Indians; frail Indian women; idiot Indians died by the hundreds on the murderous march over snow and frozen roads in that pathetic exodus. "They buried 14 or 15 at every stopping place along the way," one traveler who met them observed.

Their trail led through Nashville. Some of the men who had fought under Andrew Jackson against the Creek Indians in the War of 1812 stopped by the Hermitage to pay their respects to their old general. It was bitterest irony that he, as president, had stripped them of the land that had been theirs for centuries before the white man came to this continent.

Ross, born in 1790 near Lookout Mountain, was the son of one of those white men, a prosperous Scottish trader. One of Ross's grandfathers was a British agent among the Indians. He had married a girl who was half Cherokee. On that thin thread of Cherokee blood, Ross built his lifelong fight for the rights of the Indian.

He had grown up among them. He and his brother, Lewis Ross, were taught first by a tutor and then in a private school their father organized. Later they received some of their staunch Christian teaching in a private school where the Reverend Gideon Blackburn, pioneer Presbyterian preacher-teacher, held forth. They completed their formal education at a college in Maryville.

Better educated than many governors and presidents he corresponded with, Ross wrote with grace and dignity. No backwoods errors marked his speech, and no narrow view of the world set the Ross brothers apart from other gentlemen of the day. The letters John Ross wrote to John C. Calhoun, James Monroe, Martin Van Buren, and Governor William Carroll deepen the understanding of one of the saddest episodes in American history.

The Cherokees were not wanderers; they were farmers. When De Soto found them in the Smoky Mountains in 1540, they were cultivating their crops. They lived in cabins, not wigwams. Later, one of them, Sequoyah, put together letters from the white man's various languages to build a written language of their own. Then the Cherokees became literate. They published their own newspaper and corresponded with their agents in their own language; they established their own schools and churches and were converted to Christianity in great masses. They had a child-like trust in the white man's talk of brotherhood. "They would have become a very rare example of how aborigines could receive solid profit from the coming of the white man," historian Oliver LaFarge wrote, "had it not been for the white men's insatiable greed and utter lawlessness."

The white man's greed squeezed the Cherokee out of a fifty-thousand-square-mile territory in a corner of Tennessee, the Carolinas, Virginia, and Georgia. Little by little, by one treaty after another, the white man chipped off strips of Cherokee land. By 1787, three years before Ross's birth, one of the elder statesmen in the tribe, Hanging Maw, wrote of his disillusionment with the white man's promises. His letter is one that John Ross treasured and is among those acquired by the Tennessee State Library.

"We have held several Treaties with the Americans, when fair promises was always made that the white people should not come over [our boundary]," Hanging Maw wrote to Joseph McMinn, Indian agent who was later governor of Tennessee. "But we always find that after a treaty the white people settle much faster than before."

Hanging Maw, even as Ross, was warned against the tricky ways of the Americans. The British, the Spanish, the French— all eager to stir up trouble among the Indians against the Americans—had told the Cherokees that "the Americans only want to Deceive us," Hanging Maw wrote.

All these "people a great way off" had warned the Cherokees that if they just sat still and did nothing, all their lands would be settled by the Americans. The Americans were just as busy warning the Indians not to pay any attention to the "bad talk of the people over the great water."

"They told you lies to draw you away from your Brothers the Americans," Governor Benjamin Harrison of Virginia wrote to the Cherokees in 1782. "But we trust you will never more listen to their idle tales. We talk to you because we love you, because we are natives of the same country and expect in time to become one people. . . . " That was the promise that seemed more hopeful to Ross. He grew up in the belief that brotherly love would solve the problems.

When he was nineteen years old, in 1809, Ross was assigned his first official work for the Indians. Return J.

Meigs, U.S. Indian agent, sent him on a mission to the Cherokees, who had already drifted west.

From that date on, Ross fought for the right of the Cherokees to live on their own land. At the same time, he led them in steady loyalty to the United States—even to siding with the Americans against the Creek Indians in 1813. Almost oriental in their patience, his people held to the belief that Ross could make the white man keep his promise. They elected him "principal chief of the Cherokees" in 1828 and they kept reelecting him to that post until his death almost forty years later.

His work for the Cherokees kept him in Washington much of the time, and a good part of his correspondence is written from hotels there. "John Ross, Washington" was the only address it took to get a letter to him.

For years, he and his brother operated a store at a landing on the Tennessee River, where Chattanooga is now. But in 1828, when he and the other Cherokees were pushed out of Tennessee into Georgia, he built a mansion for his wife and eight children on the Coosa River, opposite the present city of Rome. There, with the help of many slaves, he operated a huge plantation.

In 1829, Ross wrote the secretary of war to remind him of the money promised the Cherokees in return for moving from their Tennessee land. They had ear-marked the funds for schools, Ross said, and young Indians were growing up in ignorance while they waited for the government to send the money. That same year, in another of the letters in the collection, Ross wrote Tennessee's Governor William Carroll to assure him that, in spite of all the disappointments, there was no change in the Cherokee's attitude toward the United States.

"No people could be found in the United States who would, in case of actual war, prove more loyal to the cause of the United States than the Cherokees," Ross wrote. "Yourself, as well as the President, have witnessed this fact during the late war." The Cherokees knew, he said, that President Jackson was determined to move them west. The matter had been discussed with them many times, but, Ross proclaimed, the Cherokee answer would always be "No."

Their Hands
in the Lyon's Mouth

Four times John Ross was pushed off his land to make way for the white man. Four times Ross, principal chief of the Cherokees for almost forty years, used all of his diplomatic skill to lead his people in a peaceful adjustment to the white man's demands. Four times he was told that this move would be the last, that this home would belong to the Cherokees "forever."

From the Carolina and Tennessee Smokies to middle Georgia, to north Georgia and back to Tennessee again, Ross led his people in the East. But the final exodus to Oklahoma, along the twelve-hundred-mile, grave-marked "Trail of Tears" could not be avoided. No white man has ever justified it. Historians cite no reason except the white man's greed. First it was greed for the Cherokee's farm lands, timber, hunting grounds, and then for the minerals beneath the soil.

A peace-loving people, the Cherokees as a rule fought white men only when they were provoked by violence. In John Ross's day, Cherokees—trying hard to understand the white man's God—were puzzled by the long string of broken promises. But Ross, curious mixture of Cherokee and white man, never wavered in his loyalty to the United States government. He persisted in the belief that some day the Cherokee and the U.S. citizen would live happily together.

In 1828, when the Cherokees were driven from their Tennessee lands, they settled in the Rome, Georgia, area. Ross and his brother had to give up the store they operated at Ross's Landing (now Chattanooga). He became a planter,

building a mansion for his wife and eight children and operating a huge plantation with the help of many slaves.

Ross was in Washington on Cherokee business in 1830
when word came of a new threat to their Georgia land. Gold
had been discovered on the Cherokee holdings, and Georgia
promptly "annexed" all that land. Ross protested to President Jackson that the area had been promised to the Cherokees "forever," but Georgia confiscated the Cherokee land
and distributed it by lottery. Ross hurried home to find his
mansion and all his lands taken over by white strangers.

From there, he moved the Cherokees to north Georgia, in
an area where Rossville stands today. Rossville, named later
for John Ross, was familiar to him from his boyhood when
he spent much of his time at the long, two-story log house his
grandfather, John McDonald, had built in 1797.

The house, now preserved for sight-seeing tourists, was
center of the community then. It was a stagecoach stop on
the route from Nashville to Augusta and the nearest post
office for Chattanooga citizens.

Ross was living there when word came to him of a plot
by which the Indians would be forced out of their eastern
lands entirely and moved to Oklahoma territory. Without
authorization from anybody, twenty Cherokees had signed a
"treaty" by which all Cherokees were to leave Georgia and
move to what is now Oklahoma within two years. The
"double-crossers" made the traitorous move to get more
money for their land. They paid for their treachery through
the years—some of them murdered, others forced to flee as
far away as California, afraid to return to their people.

Ross, hurrying to Washington to fight the false treaty,
took along a petition signed by seventeen thousand Cherokees. But in Washington, he got the usual run-around: from
Congress to White House to Indian Commissioner to Congress
again. He took the matter to the United States Supreme
Court, and in a letter dashed off hastily to his lawyers on

January 14, 1835, added a stoic postscript: "If you have nothing consoling to communicate, let the worst come: my mind is prepared to hear and bear anything."

Meantime, he moved his family back across the Georgia border into Tennessee, to an ancient Cherokee council place called Red Clay. In a cabin there, his family lived while he negotiated for the right to stay. Shuttling between Washington and Cherokee headquarters at Red Clay, he was a striking symbol of that moment in history when the Indian was torn between two civilizations.

At the Council House, conferring with fellow Cherokees with picturesque names like Going Snake, Crying Bird, and Major Pole Cat, Ross missed his morning newspaper. "I am secluded here in the forests and cut off from all regular communication of the mail," he wrote from Red Clay in 1835, "and my papers are received after the news of the day becomes stale." He felt caught between two duties: "Vindicating the faith and integrity of the U.S. government, as well as the rights and salvation of a weak and dependent people." And he added: "It is hard to kick against the pricks."

In 1837, when John Ross was in Washington to make a last fight to hold the Georgia territory, his brother, Lewis Ross, kept him informed of happenings among the Cherokees. United States General John E. Wool, commander of American troops in the territory, had delivered an ultimatum. He had ordered all Cherokee men to meet him in a clearing in the forest at New Echota, in what is now Dahlonega, Georgia.

All through the drenching day of February 13, 1837, some thirteen hundred Cherokees made their way across muddy fields and woods to meet Lewis Ross at the appointed spot on a river bank before nightfall. While they waited there in a pouring rain, Ross crossed to the other side for a preliminary conference with General Wool, and then made arrangements with a ferry operator to haul Indians across and back the next day. "The rain fell incessantly all night," he wrote in one of the letters in the collection of John Ross papers acquired by the manuscript section of the Tennessee State Library and Archives.

At daybreak, the rain stopped and the sun broke through. By mid-morning, 1,366 Cherokees had been hauled to the opposite shore, and they made a fearsome sight to white villagers as they marched toward the meeting ground. "As we proceeded in a solid body through the town, it was apparent that our numbers struck everybody there with astonishment," Lewis Ross wrote. General Wool, sitting on a horse, said he wanted to make a speech. "They collected as close to him as they could get," Ross described the scene. "J. Bushyhead got up on a stump and interpreted. . . . "

Substance of the speech: the Cherokees would have to leave Georgia territory by June 1838. If they did not, U.S. troops would "compel their removal." He assured them there would be "plenty of guns, buffaloes, deer," in the new land of Oklahoma. There would be "clothing and beads, blankets and other provisions." All they had to do was ask for them.

Ross said this made little impression on the Indians. "Some remarked after the speech that when they wanted blankets, they generally bought them," Ross wrote. "Others said they did not care about shoes; that shoes would blister their toes in walking." But, Ross said, they had to deal carefully with the white man. Already one of their number, Bridge Maker, had been arrested for speaking out against the fraudulent treaty. "When a people has their hands in the Lyon's mouth, prudence requires them to take it out with great care," Lewis Ross observed to his brother.

By January 1838, Lewis Ross wrote that the Cherokees knew there was no hope. "We are all labouring in great suspense to hear our final doom."

In April 1838, while John Ross was negotiating with President Van Buren about terms of removal, he was notified that the matter had been closed forever. The U.S. Supreme Court had turned down his plea that the state of Georgia be enjoined from breaking their treaty and evicting them. The court said it had no power to tell a state what to do. And so, with his Cherokee wife, Elizabeth, John Ross left his Tennessee cabin on December 4, 1838, to lead seventeen thousand Cherokees on the grueling trek to Oklahoma.

United States soldiers, under the command of General Winfield Scott, had routed Indian farmers from their fields, yanked Indian women from their kitchens, even their beds. They marched Indian children out of their schools. All were herded into stockades to await the long march west. Some Indian families were separated, never to hear of each other again. Pneumonia, dysentery, starvation felled the Cherokees as they walked, and fourteen or fifteen burials along the roadside were daily occurrences.

John Ross's wife, who was called Quatie in Cherokee, worked steadily at caring for the sick. Then she, too, suffering from exposure and exhaustion, died and was buried beside the road.

Meantime, back in the Smokies, some one thousand Cherokees who had eluded the soldiers were suffering from starvation in their hide-outs. One of them, Tsali, knew there was a price on his head.

The trouble had started the day the soldiers came to round up Tsali's family. When they hurried Tsali, his wife, children, and brother-in-law down the high ridges of the Smokies, Tsali's wife stumbled and fell. A soldier prodded her with a bayonet, and Tsali could take no more. He plotted with his relatives to fake a fall and make a get-away. One American soldier was killed in the scuffle. Tsali hastily led his family up the mountainside and hid them in the cave under Clingman's Dome, where he found scores of other Cherokees. They were still there when a message was delivered by another Indian.

General Scott was tired of trying to search out the remnant of Cherokees still in the mountains. If Tsali, the man who had killed the American soldier, would surrender, the others would be allowed to remain. Tsali, his wife, brother-in-law, and two sons were to be executed to guarantee the others the right to stay in their mountains.

Tsali did not hesitate.

"I will come," he said.

The American soldiers decided to spare Tsali's wife and younger son. The other three were offered blindfolds before the shooting. They refused. A colonel asked Tsali if he had anything to say.

"If I must be killed," he said, "I would like to be shot by my own people."

Three Cherokees carried out the orders, and the three victims were buried nearby in a grave now covered by Fontana Lake.

Some one thousand Cherokees had managed to evade the soldiers, but for years they had no land of their own. Finally, white men in the area bought some fifty-seven thousand acres in North Carolina and gave it to them as their land "forever." Unlike other Indian reservations, the one at Cherokee, North Carolina, (officially known as Qualia Boundary) is still privately owned by the Indians. Certain federal services (schools, hospitals, etc.) are furnished the tribe, which has grown to some four thousand now, but the little pocket of Cherokees in North Carolina has remained fairly free of federal control. Nestled at the southeast edge of Great Smokies National Park, the Cherokees have profited from the park tourist business. For years the dramatization of their tragic epoch, "Unto These Hills," has brought them new self-respect.

Meantime, the Cherokees who survived the death march to Oklahoma became the dominant tribe of the five Indian "nations" settling the eastern end of the state. John Ross was made principal chief of all Cherokees, in both the East and the West. He spent the rest of his life fighting for their rights, but the way was never smooth. Old feuds that had split the Cherokees when the twenty "traitors" signed their Georgia lands away in 1835 never died. During the Civil War, Cherokees on both sides used the war as an excuse to settle old scores.

Ross, a slave holder himself, tried to keep the Cherokees neutral in the white man's war. Against his advice, most of them sided with the Confederacy, and a Cherokee was the last Confederate general to surrender at the end of the war.

The vengeance the Cherokees suffered from the Union after the war was a devastating blow to them as a nation. The Union made no distinction between the Cherokees who had fought with them and those who had fought against them. Widows whose husbands had died in the Union army were punished alongside Confederate widows. John Ross, a loyal Union man, outraged at the injustice, made a resounding speech to federal officials bent on vengeance. "I had three sons in your army, also three grandsons and three nephews," the seventy-five-year-old Ross told the Yankee officers. "I have a reputation which is more to me than life. . . . "

In the state library's collection, in a letter of January 16, 1866, he wrote of his last mission to Philadelphia and Washington for the Cherokees. He was seventy-six years old then, and mentioned his "recent visit to the Cherokee Nation . . . and the long spell of sickness which the exposure of that journey brought upon me." He died in Washington on August 1, 1866, in the midst of that last mission. The treaty he fought for then was the basis of operations until the Nation was finally dissolved in 1906, and the Cherokees became United States citizens.

Ross had, by his emphasis on education, helped make them a strong force in Oklahoma—"an influence out of all proportion to their numbers," one historian said. They had become supreme court judges, lawyers, "adroit politicians at all levels."

The late Will Rogers, wit and writer, was part Cherokee. His great-aunt, Tiana Rogers, was Sam Houston's Cherokee wife after he resigned as governor of Tennessee and went to live among the Indians.

There was something about the Cherokees that set them apart from other Indians. A high percentage of them graduate from colleges, and there are poets, doctors, and scientists among them. One of John Ross's great-grandaughters is a distinguished physicist in California.

The wealth from oil on their Oklahoma land is not the whole explanation of their success, historians say. Ross pointed the way for them in 1834 when he summed up the Indians' predicament after white men touched American shores: "In knowledge, the white men were strong, for their minds were cultivated. The red men were weak, for their minds were uncultivated." The tornado had struck, and the red man's hope would be in "cultivation and acquirements of the Arts and sciences."

Fair Swap or Swindle

The mystery of Tennessee's fourth governor—the tavernkeeper who bargained with "Cherokee kings" and Chicksaw rulers to chase the last of them out of the state—still hangs heavy.

Joseph McMinn, born in Pennsylvania in 1758, was at home among the Indians, and he knew that the best time to get a message to the Cherokees was at their famed "green corn dance." He knew the protocol for making pacts with Going Snake and Path Killer; he set dates for Indian councils not by the white man's calendar, but by the "rising of the grass."

Historians have no idea how he came to be governor. He was the "man without a face" in Tennessee history until recent years, when Nashville historian Stanley Horn discovered a portrait quite by accident in a Philadelphia antique shop. But the portrait was made nineteen years before McMinn was elected governor and began pushing the Indians out of Tennessee to make room for the swelling stream of white settlers who wanted to farm the land.

The frontier governor rode through Tennessee forests in snow and in summer heat, sleeping under the trees, brewing his own medicine of forest roots to doctor his weak stomach while he dickered with the craftiest of Indian chiefs.

In 1815 McMinn became governor, and the Cherokees had flatly refused to talk to representatives of the federal government about "disposing of one foot of land." Cherokee chiefs John Ross, Path Killer, Going Snake, and Chickasatchee wrote a lengthy and indignant document to that effect.

But Joseph McMinn—plain farmer and operator of a country store—was sly enough, overbearing enough, obtuse enough to have no qualms about out-sitting and out-maneuvering the Indians. "The King and a great part of the nobility have been encamped on the South bank of Highwassey River within 1 mile of this place since the evening of the 6th," McMinn wrote on November 12, 1818. In the six days of waiting he had not had "an interview or even exchange of letters except in a few instances."

To McMinn, it was a matter of "exchanging countries," and he considered the treaty signed in July 1817 a fair swap between the Indians and Tennessee. To him, the Cherokees and Chickasaws were a "set of vagrant hunters," and he never forgave the former, "once an unprincipled foe," for fighting with the British against Americans. His own lack of principle made him one of the most hated, most feared men that the Indians had to deal with. He looked on all of them as easy victims of bribery, and he dealt with them by ultimatum.

If the Indians wanted to remain on Tennessee soil, they would have to give it up as hunting ground, McMinn told them. They would have to become citizens of the United States and "instead of following the chase for their support, pursue habits of industry and civilized life." If they insisted on continuing the hunt, they must move on beyond the boundaries of the state, farther west, on the other side of the Mississippi River. If they chose to go west, they could, according to the treaty of July 1817, have as much acreage as they had given up in Tennessee. The federal government would also bear the expense of their moving west and would present to "each poor warrior one rifle-gun and ammunition, one blanket, one brass kettle, or in lieu of the brass kettle, a beaver trap."

Path Killer and Charles Hicks, head of the whole Cherokee Nation, were never taken in by the offers of the mistrusted McMinn. McMinn had to be satisfied with the report of one of his agents that "all the old chiefs present were very much enraptured with the proposition, including Old Glass, Toochelor, the old King, and Tesstipkee. "The Path Killer and Charles Hicks were absent."

In that summer of 1817, fifty-nine-year-old Governor McMinn rode great distances in the Tennessee wilderness to sit in council with Indian chiefs and help them organize their exodus. The constant fare of spring water and whatever food was available in backwoods cabins along the way left him the victim of nagging stomach disorders. "The indisposition which I felt for some time before I parted with you continued with increased severity until Monday last," he wrote Secretary of State Daniel Graham on September 17, 1818. "During this journey to this place I was frequently compelled to dismount from my horse and make the shade of the forest trees my resting place until I became partially refreshed, and then proceed on; and what added to my misfortune was that I scarcely could eat anything which was procured for me."

McMinn warned a delegation of white men going to a council meeting with the Cherokee rulers at their own camp grounds to take their own groceries unless they were willing to take a chance on what they would get from "Cherokee House Keepers." "I am doubtful they will furnish anything but Beef and Bread (perhaps coffee). Bacon and butter . . . will form no part of the ration. . . . Flour and spirits can be had here with convenience."

In the same letter McMinn reported a "green corn dance" being given by the Cherokees and the "talk" that he sent ahead by a runner to the assemblage—all aimed at hurrying the Indians out of the territory. McMinn personally undertook taking a census of the Indians willing to make the exchange of land. "Suffering cold and hardship, with a very small share of health," he got up at 4:00 A.M. to take care of his official correspondence, and he worked on his records until two o'clock the next morning. "I have invited them to

attend and Draw provisions, which has been done," he wrote
in November 1818. "I am constantly employed in enrolling
and fitting out those who are ready to embark for the West.
. . . Our number of families now amount to nearly 900 including 146 who have taken reservations, and are daily aug-
menting."

McMinn gloated over winning over to his scheme the
nephew of Charles Hicks, arch foe of the white man:

> I am at this moment (9 o'clock at night) called from
> my quarters to walk about half a mile to enter into a
> contract in secret for the purpose of enrolling the Neph-
> ew of Charles Hicks, who is married into a family nearly
> first in number and rank, from which I derive great con-
> solation, particularly as they all live in the immediate
> vicinity of Charles Hicks.

Patiently McMinn parceled out the terms of the treaty to
the Indians, giving them days to discuss it among themselves
before he presented the next point. "I occupied their attention for nearly three hours on yesterday in reading and explaining," he wrote, "and today I have promised to send
them a long written Talk, in which I shall come to a point
where I will halt; they will learn this day that, if the Boon is
to be theirs, they must surrender their Possession & claim to
the United States."

McMinn complained of the "hurry, bustle & noise of a
disorderly multitude who can only be kept in bounds by
military force" and of the "immense weight of business in
purchasing . . . boats, stores, equipping vast numbers to sail
for the west. . . . Not less than $30,000 will have Passed thro
my hands since I came here, and before I can depart, for all
of which duplicate receipts must be taken—the greater part in
my own hand writing."

In December 1818, the weary governor was still among
the Cherokees, getting up at 4:00 A.M. and working through
the night. "At half past 2 A.M. I set down to advise that I am

yet alive," he wrote Tennessee's secretary of state. "Since the adjournment of the conference I have been industriously engaged in Paying the emigrants for improvements & arrangements for their embarkation to the West. . . .This course will lead to a conclusion in a few days and enable me to return to the more retired walks of life, which I assure you will be no less pleasing to my mind than beneficial to my health."

Retirement, however, at the end of his three terms as governor in 1821, did not turn out to be the blissful thing McMinn had visualized. He bought a one-hundred acre farm in Hawkins County and twenty slaves to work it, but his third wife refused to accompany him there.

For two years Governor McMinn had been married to his third wife, who was a widow and the mother of Colonel Willoughby Williams who recorded much of Nashville's history. McMinn had been away from home for months at a time as he worked among the Indians, and his wife had remained in Nashville. When she refused to leave her Nashville relatives to accompany him to Hawkins County, he petitioned the legislature for a divorce in October 1821. When it was granted, he "returned every article of property which came into my hands by this marriage, and gave her $2,000 out of my estate."

The 63-year-old retired governor, thrice widowed, was sad contrast to the hopeful young Joseph McMinn who had followed his brother to Tennessee thirty-four years before. Born of Quaker parents in 1758, McMinn had left his native Pennsylvania and bought his first Hawkins County farm in 1787. He was twenty-nine years old then, married, and the father of a one-year-old daughter, Jane. Neighbors recalled seeing this first of his three wives working alongside McMinn in the fields, and it is assumed they accumulated enough property to give him some weight in government affairs.

He had not been in Tennessee three years when he joined the Hawkins County militia, and he was major in the militia by the time he was thirty-five. He was also justice of the peace.

When Hawkins County sent five delegates to the convention in Knoxville in 1796 to write the state constitution, McMinn was one of them. It was January 11 when he sat down at the conference table with Andrew Jackson, James Robertson, and fifty-two other delegates, and a month later they had finished the job. On February 9, 1796, he was sent to the federal capitol in Philadelphia to deliver Tennessee's constitution, and he was instructed to stay there until he was assured that Tennessee congressmen would be allowed to sit in Congress.

It was then that McMinn took time to have his portrait painted. It is probable that he met George Washington, as president, or John Adams, as vice-president, while he was in Philadelphia, and he chose the same artist, Rembrandt Peale, who had painted Washington's portrait. When Stanley Horn stumbled across the painting almost one hundred fifty years later, he found it signed with the complete identification: "Major Joseph McMinn, painted at Philadelphia. 1796. R. P. pinxit."

McMinn was thirty-eight years old when the portrait was painted, and when he came back from Philadelphia he was promoted to the rank of colonel in the militia. He was elected to all but one of the first six terms of the legislature, and he was Speaker of the senate for his last three terms.

Then family sorrows began to accumulate for McMinn. His first wife died while he was Speaker of the senate, in 1811, and the following year the fifty-four-year-old McMinn married eighteen-year-old Rebecca Kincade, daughter of a farmer neighbor. Only three years later Rebecca died of a "nervous fever," on January 11, 1815, and two weeks after that, on January 27, his daughter Jane died.

McMinn was still bowed in grief when a delegation of fellow citizens came the following July to ask him to run for governor. In a letter to his brother-in-law, telling of the death of his wife and daughter, McMinn told of the bid that had come to him to announce for governor: "I wished to spend the balance of my days in retirement," the bereaved man wrote. "But to my utter astonishment, on the 6th day of July, a very lengthy address was handed me from a large and respectable class of my fellow citizens soliciting me to offer for governor of Tenn. Having been frequently chided for leaving my countries service, I thought I would give my name and did so, and wonderful to tell, I was elected in twenty-six days." Nobody ever referred to him as a powerful orator, a skilled politician, a brainy man. Yet the size of his victories was staggering. Five men—including a congressman, a senator, and various state officials—were competing for the job, and McMinn won twice as many votes as any of his opponents. Two years later he almost doubled the vote gained by his one opponent, and for his third term his vote was almost three times as large as that of his opponent.

Whether McMinn was already known for his shrewdness in dealing with the Indians—and the Indian problem was a pressing one at the time—is not clear. Certainly much of his energy in his six years as governor was devoted to shoving the Indians out of Tennessee as rapidly as possible.

His poor business judgment almost wrecked the young state's banking system. He was known as a "slow, conscientious, painstaking officer . . . essentially a man of the present tense . . . and without any of the powers of concentration which enable more gifted minds to forecast the future." When his six years as governor were finished and he had retired to his Hawkins County farm, McMinn saw nothing undignified in running a tavern and grocery store there. Tennesseans were humiliated to have travelers snicker at the spectacle of a former governor "bustling about the tavern, at once landlord, barkeeper and head waiter, administering entertainment to guests of every degree."

But the restless bargainer was soon back in harness again, dickering with the Indians when he died at Cherokee headquarters on November 17, 1824. He and General R. J. Meigs "were commissioners on the part of the United States to negotiate a treaty with the Cherokees and had their head-quarters at the Indian agency . . . where the town of Charleston now stands," one historian reported. "The Governor . . . while writing at his desk fell back stricken with dropsy of the heart. . . . His faithful body servant Dave, the only person present when he died."

Death came three years after McMinn left the governor's office, and he was sixty-six years old. His grave in a country graveyard on the banks of the Hiwassee River was long un-marked, overgrown with vines, leaving no more record of his passing that way than the Indians whom he had ushered out of the green hills and into the swamps of Arkansas. His will, strange and uninspired as many of his transactions, stated that the sister of his dead wife was to receive a set of spoons; a nephew was to inherit a fur hat.

Punishment on the Unforgiving Frontier

Cutting off a man's ears was the least painful part of the punishment for a horse thief when Nashville was a frontier town "out West." Hot branding irons seared the emblem of the crime into his flesh. Thirty-nine lashes on the bare back, "well laid on" at the whipping post on the courthouse grounds, drew the blood and left ugly scars. For a man's crops and even his life depended on his horse, and stealing a horse was the worst of frontier crimes.

John McKain, Jr., the first horse thief convicted in a Nashville court, was aware of that on the Saturday morning in May 1793, when he stood before Judge John McNairy to hear the sentence. The case had been pending for almost two years, after McKain was first tried for stealing from Aquilla Carmack, on July 15, 1790, "one bay mare with a star in her forehead and branded on the mounting shoulder with IH."

When the guilty verdict was announced, McKain was asked if he had anything to say in his own behalf. He "saith nothing," the county court clerk wrote in a huge leather-bound book that circuit court clerk Alf Rutherford kept locked in a glass case in 1965. So Judge McNairy pronounced the dreadful sentence:

That you stand in the Pillory one hour, be whipped on your Bare Back, with 39 lashes, and that you be Branded on the right cheek with the letter H, of the length of three-quarters of an inch and the breadth of half an inch, and on the left cheek with the letter T, of the same demention as the letter H, in a plain and visible manner, and that both ears be cut off and that the Sher-riff of Davidson put this sentence in action immediately.

The pillory was a wooden stock, or frame, with a hole cut out for the prisoner to stick his head through and holes on either side to lock his hands in place. There he stood helpless while fellow citizens looked on in contempt or shouted insults.

The same week that McKain got his punishment for steal-ing a horse, the first woman convicted of a crime in Davidson County was stripped to the waist for lashes on the back at the whipping post. Elizabeth Moser, wife of Christian Moser, had been convicted of petit larceny. The court record stated that on April 15, 1792, she "stole 6 pounds of soape of the value of two pence, and three ounces of sewing thread" from James Hutcherson.

When the case was tried in May 1793, Judge McNairy "ordered therefore that the said Elizabeth Moser be taken to the Publick Whipping Post, and there receive on the Bair Back nine lashes *well laid on* and that the Sheriff of Davidson put this sentence in Execution immediately."

Nashville was in North Carolina then, as was all the pres-ent state of Tennessee. Cases from both Davidson and Sumner counties (and later Robertson and Smith) were tried in the Nashville court. The court met twice a year, usually convening on the first Monday of May and November.

At the first meeting of the Superior Court of Law and Equity there in November 1788, Judge McNairy got things off to a stern start. "He made a proclamation," the clerk wrote in careful script on thick pages now browning with age and potted with worm holes, "commanding silence under pain of imprisonment, while the Judge proceeded on the Publick ruling."

At that first meeting of court, on the first Monday in November 1788, a young lawyer named Andrew Jackson was granted permission to practice law in Nashville. In fact, the

Judge said, since there was no one else around to do it, he would ask Jackson to act as prosecuting attorney when one was needed. That arrangement would be in force, the judge said, "until this court can be fitted with a sufficient number of other attorneys regularly admitted." The next year Jackson was appointed to the job on a regular basis.

The sheriff at that time was having troubles with the jail. "Thomas Hickman, high Sheriff for Davidson County, came into Court and protested against the sufficiency of the Publick Gaol," the clerk recorded in 1788.

Top men of the day strode through the doors of the little log courthouse, as lawyers, litigants, members of the jury. General James Winchester, revolutionary war hero and builder of the fortresslike Cragfont in Sumner County, was called to serve on the first jury, and so was Robert Weakley, famed Indian fighter and legislator. Other juries of the day included men like pioneer Kaspar Mansker, colorful innkeeper Thomas Talbot, and political leader John Bell.

Untangling claims to the vast new lands was a massive legal puzzle. The list of men who sued and were sued reads like a *Who's Who* of early Tennessee.

Timothy Demonbreun, French trader who was among the first to settle in Nashville, sued Anthony Crutcher for not delivering a slave he had paid for. William Blount, governor of the territory before Tennessee became a state, showed up as executor of an involved estate. Abram Maury, for whom Maury County was named, was excused from jury duty because of illness. James Robertson, one of the founders of Nashville, was sued over a property settlement. Valentine Sevier, brother of John Sevier, first governor of Tennessee, and Stockley Donelson, brother of the future Mrs. Andrew Jackson, were involved in lawsuits.

John Overton, who later helped plot Jackson's rise to the White House, began his law practice in the Nashville court alongside Jackson. William Cocke, later a United States senator, and Randal McGavock were soon admitted to the bar there. Willie Blount, who was to be fourth governor of the state, was involved in a land dispute with John Deaderick. Archibald Roane, who was to become second governor of the state, was one of the judges.

There was hardly a man in the courthouse who had not fought in the Revolutionary War. And independence was so shiningly new that court records were dated not only "in the year of Our Lord," but also "in the year of Our Independence."

But English customs and English money were still used. The first case on record in Nashville involved Timothy Demonbreun's suit for an unpaid bill, and the court ordered payment of "12 ½ per cent on 34 pounds, eight shillings." Not until 1795, in a case involving a plaintiff named River Jordan, were fines settled in dollars.

England seemed far away, though, four years after the first court met in Nashville. It was the first Monday in November 1792, the regular day for fall court to convene. But they had barely met before they adjourned, that same day.

Indians had raided Zeigler's Station in Sumner County the June before, and on the last day of September the Creeks had swept down on Buchanan's Station, near Nashville. Men venturing out of the latter stockade to do farmwork had been scalped in full view of women peeping from the fortress, and in some cases the Indians had cut off the victim's head and mounted it on a pole to carry high in triumph.

"The Indians were so troublesome on the Frontier about this time that the Court and Jury thought it most advisable to adjourn court," the clerk recorded hurriedly. When he had closed the book, he must have been in a quandary about where to keep it safe from the Indians. The fact that it survives today as one of the county's invaluable sources of information is remarkable.

Even stealing a handkerchief was a crime to take to court then. In May 1794, John Bradly of Nashville was convicted of that crime and was "taken to the Publick Whipping Post to receive on his Bare Back 39 lashes well laid on." Whippings were more practical punishment in pioneer days than imprisonment, historians point out, because a man could be whipped and go back to his work. Laborers were too scarce to have them shut up in jail.

Nobody became unduly alarmed at fierce fights among frontier laborers, and sentences were light. On May 6, 1794, Isaac Roberts and Robert Evans "had a dispute and fought, the event of which terminated in said Evans biting off the lower end of said Roberts' right ear." Court records said that "sufficient proof was introduced to establish the fact that the witness saw the part of the ear of said Roberts in the mouth of said Evans," but never stated the outcome of the case.

William Hawthorne accused John Rains of assault "with swords, knives, nails, fingers and fists." For this "great damage" Rains was fined sixpence, and another sixpence in court costs.

In 1798, "in the 23rd year of American Independence," Andrew Jackson became judge of the court, serving with Archibald Roane and David Campbell. These three were the judges in 1800 when Andrew Pierce, laborer, of Robertson County, was convicted of stealing "one sorrell mare branded on the near Buttock thus C, of the value of 40 dollars, and one year-old colt of the value of 50 dollars" from John Chowning. The sentence added a new twist in torture: "That the said Andrew Pierce shall stand in the pillory one hour, and shall be publicly whipped on his bare back with 39 lashes well laid on, and at the same time shall have both his ears nailed to the pillory and cut off, and shall be branded with the letter T, etc."

Stealing Negroes was as frequent a crime as stealing horses. Joseph Barnes was fined two hundred dollars in 1798 for "seducing, enticing and persuading Negroes out of the possession of David Vaughn and his wife Susannah and harbouring the same." John Walker was fined three hundred fifty dollars in 1801 for "slave stealing," taking the "female slave named Peggy, aged 17," the property of William Gunn.

The first divorce case came before the court on November 21, 1800, when May Parker sued Nathaniel Parker. No grounds were mentioned in the record, but the divorce was granted.

Murder was inconsequential, compared to burglary and horse stealing. John Childrup, who "maliciously struck" John Regan with a "plank of oak wood on the left temple and above the left eye" and killed him, was convicted of manslaughter in November 1801. The sentence was that "the said Childrup be burned on his left hand with the letter M."

Andrew Jackson and Hugh L. White, later justice of the state supreme court, were judges then. In the November 1801 session, they handed down the death sentence for the first time—once for horse stealing, once for burglary. It was thirteen years after the first court opened that capital punishment began in Davidson County.

Henry Baker, convicted of stealing "one brown gelding, about 15 hands high, about 6 years old . . . of value of $120" from Richard Harmon, was sentenced to be "hanged by the neck until he is dead . . . on Tuesday, the 29th of December . . . at the Publick Gallows."

The grimmest day listed in the thick book of many sorrows is June 25, 1802, when three horse thieves were hanged in the course of one afternoon. They were Charles Powel, a laborer from Smith County, to be hanged between noon and 2:00 P.M.; Michael West of Sumner County, to be hanged between noon and 3:00 P.M.; and Samuel Black of Sumner County, to be hanged between noon and 4:00 P.M.

While the three horse thieves dangled from the gallows in the summer sun, three brothers who had been tried for murder by the same court that tried the thieves went free. The three brothers were accused of killing one Henry Dillard "with a leaden bullet . . . from a rifle gun." Jacob and Matthew Bethany, who admittedly "aided and abetted in the murder," were acquitted. Thomas Bethany, the brother who pulled the trigger, was convicted, but his sentence was to "be burned in the left hand with the letter M." One glove could hide his guilt forever.

He'd Rather Fight
Than Crop

Hardly a hippie, heroic Thomas Butler faced a court-martial rather than have his hair cut. And nobody could have predicted the troubles that fight would bring on.

A tall, handsome man with hair grown "gray in the service of his country," Colonel Butler had fought in the Revolutionary War and heard no complaint then about the length of his hair, worn in a ponytail. Years after that war and many other painful campaigns in the service of his country, he had no intention of giving in to the army's orders, in 1803, to cut his hair.

George Washington's hair, tied in a queue at the back of his neck, had met with no disapproval when he led the army. Neither had there been criticism of Thomas Jefferson and other patriots who helped create the nation—no matter how long they wore their hair. It was George Washington, in fact, who first sent Butler to Tennessee, to see that white settlers did not take over the land assigned the Indians. There Butler and Andrew Jackson became close friends; their wives visited each other on their neighboring farms, and the Butler children were often in the Jackson home. Eventually, in fact, Butler's oldest son, Robert, married Rachel Jackson's favorite niece, Rachel Hays. But that romance came long after the haircut hassle.

Jackson backed Butler in his insistence that he had the right not to cut his hair. Jackson was at that time major general of the Tennessee militia. His advice was doubly valuable because he was not only a lawyer and a military man; he had also served as United States senator and had been a judge on the state supreme court.

Jackson, who would become president twenty-seven years later, did not hesitate to advise Colonel Butler to take the hair cropping matter straight to the White House. Thomas Jefferson was president, and, as fighter for independence, he would certainly come to the aid of the colonel who wanted to keep his hair unshorn.

Army regulations had been changed on April 30, 1801, to require officers to "crop their hair." Colonel Butler, serving under General James Wilkinson—one of the shadiest characters in American history—ignored the order, and Wilkinson began making threats. He let Butler know he would wreck his military career if Butler did not "leave the tail behind."

On August 7, 1803, Jackson wrote President Jefferson to ask him to bring a halt to Wilkinson's persecution of the distinguished Colonel Butler. The United States, growing up now with its acquisition of the Louisiana territory, would look silly if it brought one of its fine officers to trial over as ridiculous a thing as a ponytail, Jackson argued. "The golden moment when all the Western Hemisphere rejoices at the Joyfull news of the cession of Louisiana we hope will not be marred by the scene of an aged and meritorious officer before a court martial for the disobedience of an order to deprive him of the gift of nature worn by him both for ornament and convenience," Jackson wrote the president.

Butler's courtesy and courage had made him a hero with fellow soldiers and with Indians. "Sir, the removal of such an officer for his well known attachment to his locks, gray in the service of his country, opens a door for the greatest tyranny," Jackson added.

But Jefferson was not moved by Jackson's letter. Wilkinson began his campaign against Butler by separating him from his family, sending him to New Orleans to take troops there in the height of the yellow fever season. Jackson advised Butler to be on his way quickly, so that Wilkinson could not hold any delay against him. So Butler left Nashville—forever, as it turned out—on Tuesday, August 28, 1804.

Jackson promised he would have a petition signed "by all the respectable citizens of this District, and forwarded to the President." The army's high-handed way of dealing with a man's hair style didn't sound like the kind of democracy Butler had fought for. It wasn't the hair so much, it was the principle of the thing. If necessary, Jackson would take it to a court-martial, to the president, to the Congress. Both Jackson and Butler were well aware of the political battle behind the ponytail fight.

Wilkinson, a thoroughly slippery character who had been in and out of one disgraceful scheme after another, had been in the pay of Spain while he represented this country. It was he who schemed against this country and later laid the blame on Aaron Burr. Hard drinking and habitual greed and cheating had made him one of the most despised, and most powerful, men in the country for years. He hated a man he could not control. Butler was aware of Wilkinson's ingrigue with Spain, and Wilkinson knew it. The threat to Butler's ponytail was Wilkinson's way of getting at him.

Wilkinson's revenge in sending Butler on an overland journey to New Orleans in August was bad enough. When Butler arrived there in early October 1804, he found the city so raging with yellow fever that he dared not take his troops closer than eight miles from the city.

Butler wrote Wilkinson that he would not budge from his stand: "I shall not cut my hair." The president kept silent, and so did the secretary of war, Henry Dearborn. (Jefferson had won the lifelong hatred of Aaron Burr from the time he maneuvered him out of the presidency in 1800; Jefferson had been on the side of Wilkinson ever since the latter turned on Aaron Burr.)

The collection of Andrew Jackson letters now being assembled and edited at the Hermitage in Nashville is rich in insights into the controversy. Neither Jackson nor Butler ever wavered in the determination to take the fight to Congress, if necessary. "Surely the President will not tamely look on and see an officer baren down this way," Butler wrote Jackson. "If so, then I have faithfully served my country for nothing." For an army officer fifty years old, whose greatest pride had been in helping establish a free country, that was a bitter statement. His father was a general, and his brothers were distinguished officers.

Butler then asked Jackson to pass along a message to Mrs. Butler. "Impress on her mind the necessity of bearing up against these momentary evils," the optimistic Butler concluded the letter.

A few weeks later, on December 17, 1804, Butler wrote that the poor mail service, from both Washington and Nashville, had him frantically awaiting every delivery, even until the post office closed at 10:00 P.M. He had asked the secretary of war for a "speedy trial," but had no word in reply. He kept his spirits reasonably high, however.

On Christmas Eve, 1804, in New Orleans, far from his family, Butler wrote his Christmas greeting to Jackson and his wife, adding the news that he had received a note from Wilkinson, but no word of when the trial would be held. "He means to oppress me by procrastination."

Obviously Wilkinson had lined up Tennessee's congressmen against Butler, for not one of them answered his letters. By January 28, 1805, Butler had evidence that mail bags arriving in New Orleans from Washington were being cut open on the way and "sundry letters to me from the City of Washington had been cut out." Wilkinson had his agents everywhere.

Butler said he knew that by now both the president and the secretary of war had made definite decisions against him. "I am too proud to sink under this persecution," Butler wrote, "and a day of retribution must come round, and that before long. I feel more for Mrs. Butler and my family than for myself."

Two weeks later Mrs. Butler died suddenly, and it was Jackson's duty to notify Butler on February 11, 1805. Butler, frantic to get back to Tennessee to see his children and make arrangements for "Capt. Purdy to carry on the farm work while I am away," wrote Wilkinson and the secretary of war for permission to return to Tennessee, at least briefly. Both of them ignored his request.

March 4, 1805, Butler wrote Jackson and asked him to keep an eye on "my little orphan family." By August 1805, there was a second death in Butler's family. His mother-in-law died, and Butler asked permission to return to Tennessee to settle the estate. His request was ignored.

In July 1805, Butler stood trial. The court-martial, held in New Orleans, lasted from July 1 to July 10. Wilkinson's charges seemed fantastic to Butler. He accused Butler of "wilfull, obstinate and continued disobedience of the General Order of the 30th of April, 1801, for regulating the cut of the hair."

Wilkinson also accused Butler of "Mutinous Conduct, in appearing publicly in command of the Troops at the City of New Orleans with his hair cued." Wilkinson recommended that Butler be "suspended from all command, pay and Emoluments for the space of twelve Calendar Months." The court adjourned on July 10, and then began the long wait to see what the decision would be.

Reflecting on the whole matter on August 26, 1805, Butler wrote Jackson that his only reason for going through the long ordeal was to eventually get his case before Congress. He felt the regulations about haircuts were an "arbitrary infraction of my natural right."

He felt confident after the trial that the persecution he

had suffered for almost two years would rouse the indignation of "every independent and virtuous American." He wondered that our country, barely twenty-nine years out of the grip of England, would so easily give in to dictatorship. "Shall we never assume a national character?" he wrote Jackson. "Are we to be eternally goaded with the customs of Europe?"

It angered him that Wilkinson, in the trial, had cited a German soldier of fortune, one Marshal Saxe of Saxony, who had laid down laws about how his soldiers should have "their heads shorn, and wear Black or Gray lambskin caps." On top of that, Wilkinson had circulated the story in New Orleans that President Jefferson had cut off his own long locks to show that he thought Wilkinson was right in the controversy. Butler thought that if the president had cropped his hair, it was not for that reason.

Butler sent a complete copy of the court-martial charges to Jackson. He said he felt compelled to "throw as much light as possible on a subject founded in tyranny," to keep Jackson posted on "this unprecedented persecution."

Those two letters of August 26, 1805—one about family matters and one about the trial—are the last from Butler in the Jackson collection. Two weeks after Butler wrote those letters, he was dead. He had gone to a friend's plantation a few miles from New Orleans for a visit, caught a cold that soon developed a high fever and died four days later, on September 8, 1805.

He had not heard the results of the court-martial. But he died uncompromised. His locks were fiercely, proudly unshorn.

Judgment Day on the Frontier

Judgment Day came early for Tennessee's pioneer church members. They didn't have to wait till the hereafter to get their punishment.

When they slipped from the "straight and narrow"—precisely described by each congregation—they "caught Hell" right here on earth. If they so much as danced to a fiddle or used a "cussword," they could be summoned before the church elders or deacons sitting as a court.

Punishment could be swift and harsh—everything from an embarrassing public confession to banishment from the church. Either could brand a man, or a woman, for life.

Often church trials handled matters which would be referred to civil courts today. Out of the old church records now being collected by the manuscripts division of the Tennessee State Library and Archives come stories of members tried because they mistreated their slaves, committed adultery, murdered, stole, drank to excess, lied, claimed land that was not theirs, played cards and fought on Sunday, gambled, attended dances, failed to pay their bills, or charged too much for their corn.

At Zion Presbyterian Church in Maury County, for example, rules were rigid. On the Sabbath, there was to be no shaving, no cooking, no chopping wood, no visiting, except to the sick, and no activity except attending church and instructing slaves.

When a lady member of the church was charged with being drunk in 1813, it rocked Zion Church almost out of its log walls. The close-knit group of families who made up the congregation had left their native South Carolina just six years before. First thing they did after they hacked their way through the canebrake south of Columbia was to build their church. It was the stern center of their lives.

George, one of the founding members, for instance, said he felt duty-bound to bring the drunkenness charge against his sister-in-law, Charlotte. He had seen her drunk, he said, and he could prove it. In April 1813, the church elders met to hear the case. They had tried in vain to bring about a reconciliation between the two parties, both members of leading families.

"The accuser persisted in accusing and the accused stubbornly denied," the church clerk recorded the proceedings. George charged that Charlotte's "reason was impaired by drinking spirits."

George testified first. He told about the day he was summoned to his sister-in-law's home by her servants. Her husband was away on business, and, the servants said, "Miss Charlotte" had suffered a fall and was "very bad hurt." George was horrified at what he saw: Charlotte in bed, and the room reeking of whiskey, a half-empty glass of whiskey on the bedside table, Charlotte nauseated, and her tongue so thick that he couldn't get the straight of it when she tried to tell what had happened.

During the church trial, George admitted there had been "bad feeling" between him and his sister-in-law. He admitted he had been spying on her, trying to catch her buying more whiskey than the medicinal needs of the household required. He admitted that she seemed too ill to get out of bed the day he called.

Then it was Charlotte's turn to testify. The trouble began as she was coming from the potato patch, she said, and had to climb a rail fence. Her long skirts somehow got caught on the rails, and she suffered a terrible fall, pulling the top rail down on top of herself and landing across two other rails.

Expecting a child soon, she was "deathly sick"—nauseated and unable to move for a while. Somehow, at length, she got up and made her way across the field, into the house, and to bed. At first she thought she could withstand the shock without alarming anyone. She poured herself a stiff drink of whiskey, the only medicine in the house. By the time her brother-in-law and his wife arrived, she had consumed half a glass of whiskey.

The next witness was Charlotte's husband, who had never known her to be intoxicated, he said. Then one after another of the ladies in the family testified. None of them had ever seen her intoxicated. George's wife said she had never known Charlotte to be drunk, but she had thought she was in labor the day of the accident.

The church elders were dismayed. They were not only chagrined that Charlotte had been brought to trial, but they dismissed all charges against her with a glowing tribute, ordering that "she be considered . . . of fair and unblemished character." The elders ruled George "deficient in point of Christian caution and circumspection" and "admonished him to act more cautiously in the future." At which George stalked out, announcing that he would "silently withdraw until I am better satisfied."

Historians today gain vivid insight into pioneer life by studying the old church records. Out of the minutes come stories that show the concern of members for their community, acts of charity toward the needy, a constant program of education, and concern for man's brutality.

At Zion Presbyterian, in the pre-Civil War days, there was the case of the horse-whipped slave boy named Arch, in March 1825. Word of the cruel treatment of the lad emerged at prayer meeting about a week after the incident. The slave owner, Mr. L., who had committed the crime, was a member of the church. The congregation was outraged.

Two members were appointed to investigate the next morning. It was a cold March morning, and the boy was lying on a pile of fodder on the floor of a log cabin without any door. He was so sore from his wounds he could hardly move. He had been whipped with 150 whacks of a paddle and 150 lashes of a cowhide whip "on his naked hips, back and thighs." The wounds from the paddling were still raw, and the deep stripes from the rawhiding were forming scabs.

The church elders, summoning all witnesses and the slave-owner, held the trial in April 1825. The owner's answers were often evasive:

Question: Did the scabs appear deep?

Answer: I could not tell.

Q: Do scars seem inflamed?

A: They were raw at the time I saw him.

Q: Did he have fever?

A: I did not examine his pulse.

Mr. L. felt entirely justified in the "punishment" of his runaway slave. This was the second time the boy had run away, he said. The master had not punished him the first time, but he told the boy that if it happened again he would lay on the paddle and the whip—a hundred strokes each, plus ten more for each day the boy was absent.

Arch, "an insolent boy," a troublemaker, was away for five days the second time. His master testified that he whipped the boy "not in passion, but in consequence of serious reflection on the subject," that he had done it "out of a sense of duty."

One witness testified:

Q: In what position did Mr. L. place his boy to receive the punishment?

A: He had him tied across a log, with his feet fastened to stakes.

How long had Mr. L. given the boy to recover from the whipping? He had put him to work the day after the church brethren visited him. Though the boy "could not rise without great pain and difficulty," he was put to work "removing stones from about the house." The master said he "thought the work would be an advantage to the boy."

The elders' decision: the master "had great provocation from the conduct of his boy," and they believed he had "performed the punishment as a conscientious discharge of duty," but they thought he had "made a rash promise and . . . the punishment exceeded the bounds of propriety." With a warning "to be more careful in the future in making such promises and in inflicting such punishment," they dismissed the case.

Negroes were members of the church from the first. They were baptized there, took communion there, were held responsible for all church regulations, just as their white brethren were. Some of them were elders in the church. Slave owners were specifically "requested to use all means which expedience and duty may warrant for their [the slaves'] instruction, especially on the Sabbath," by act of the elders on September 22, 1834. From the first, the white elders judged their black brothers with special consideration.

On June 14, 1815, four slaves, Prince and Judy, Moses and Venus, were charged with adultery, "pilfering and lying," and fornication. Each admitted his own guilt, "professed sorrow for it, and promised to endeavor to amend his life in the future." The elders, pondering the matter, said they "supposed the peculiar situation of these people may authorize us to adopt a treatment a little varying from the common mode." They instructed the four penitents to "publicly acknowledge their faults before the congregation of Black people on next Sabbath two weeks." Then they would be on probation until the fall sacrament: "If a good report is given of them, they will be received into the church again. But if there should be still bad reports against their character, they will be rejected."

According to church records, they were not rejected. But there were other church members—some of them among the most prominent in the congregation—who were thrown out, often for "excessive use of spirits."

One of the bitterest controversies to come before the church involved the young minister and an elder, who was old and bent "with rheumatism and petulant at the time." The minister boarded at the elder's home, and had not paid his board. The minister, in turn, said he had not been paid his salary, and charged the elder with "intemperance, falsehood, and indecent language . . . and addressing me two most insulting and uncalled for letters . . . in suing me for board."

The elder's letter had a ring familiar today: "As I am nothing but an 'Old Fogy' (the most respectful epithet you ever could apply to me), I suppose you think I have no use for money or ever trying to collect my own; 'Old Fogyism' trys to incur no more liabilities than it has the means to meet; 'young America' goes upon the principle *buy, buy,* but never pay unless the law compels you."

The case was referred to the presbytery of all Maury County, and they decided against the crotchety elder. The next year both he and the penniless preacher were dead.

But if Zion Presbyterian Church, five miles south of Columbia, was "practically the Supreme Court of the community" before the Civil War, so were other Presbyterian and Primitive Baptist churches in their areas.

In Williamson County, the Wilson Creek Primitive Baptist Church began keeping records at its first service on October 13, 1804, and recorded every service and business meeting to the present day.

One of the ministers of the church was involved in a long series of controversies with a member of the congregation, and the latter accused him of using "abuseful language" in

October 1816. "He treated me with insolence at Esq. Shelbourne's," the church member charged. "On the next day at his own meeting house, he there called me one of the meanest men in the world and a hypocrite sliding through the world and keeping himself hid, and he also called Brother S. an ignorant fool and a hypocrite besides."

The minister refused to acknowledge any error, and was at length thrown out of the church. From time to time he was readmitted, but repeatedly caused friction.

Church membership was a highly prized privilege, and members, once thrown out, usually worked hard at getting reinstated. One man, charged with an unethical transaction in a business matter in May 1830, confessed all and begged another chance. "I did not intend to do injustice in that act, but if I did, I beg forgiveness," the accused brother pleaded. "My fellowship in the church is dear to me."

In November 1850, when two prominent members of the congregation locked horns over the dividing line between their property, the church labored long to bring about a reconciliation. One of the parties, Brother Tom, accused his neighbor, Nat, of "taking rails belonging to me and enclosing a part of said strip of land as his own." On protest, Brother Nat moved the fence to where it had been, but refused any settlement of the disagreement.

For days the church took testimony from both sides. They sent surveyors and deacons to check all claims. At last they seemed near a settlement of the difficulty when Brother Nat "arose from his seat and said he was persecuted like a partridge in the mountains and asked the brethren to pray for him; he put on his hat and with hasty steps went out of the house."

It was six months later before the church, after many sessions of "laboring hard with those brethren until a late hour in the evening," settled the matter. Nat was the guilty party, they said. "And he done wrong when he said he was pursued like a partridge in the mountains and left the House," the deacons concluded.

Much depended, in the decisions, on the attitude of the accused. If he seemed earnestly penitent, the church was usually lenient. But there were cases of harsh humiliation of the sinner. At Jerusalem Cumberland Presbyterian Church in McMinn County, on March 31, 1833, a young woman was accused of fornication. The church elders advised her to write a confession and send it to them. "The substance of some rumors that are out on me are true," she wrote. "If I know my heart at all, I assure you I have repented." At which the elders promptly suspended her from the church and voted to read her confession to the assembled congregation.

One of the most frequent "sinners" to show up in church records was Archibald, member of Cave Creek Primitive Baptist Church in Roane County, who once even accused himself. He "laid in charges against himself for intoxication" in January 1837, and the church "forgave him on his own acknowledgement." But in 1847, Brother Archibald was in trouble for betting. He was charged with "swalling [swallowing] a crawfish for a pair of shoes and for other unchristian and disorderly conduct." The church "declared nonfellowship against him."

Intoxication was the most frequent charge in the churches. Adultery ranked next, and property fights were common. Few cases between church members ever reached civil courts.

Many of the trials involved church regulations, everything from arguments over church doctrine to dancing. In New Providence Cumberland Presbyterian Church, in McNairy County, in February 1847, one member was charged with "permitting a party to fiddle and dance in his house, which he acknowledged." At that same session, there was a charge against another member for "taking an active part, several times, in dancing after the fiddle, which he acknowledges." When all of the accused at the dances had shown "submission and humiliation and made confession," they were allowed "to continue their membership."

Mars Hill Presbyterian Church at Athens was harsh on drinkers and dancers. In 1845, one of their members, at the auction sale of his father's property, "was seen to frequently follow the bottle into the house." Another member saw the same man "drinking at my own corn-husking last fall and at other times under the influence of free drinking." He was "suspended from the privileges of the church."

A well-educated doctor and his wife moved to the community and joined Mars Hill Presbyterian Church before they realized its unyielding ways. In December 1838, when the church objected to the fact that the doctor and his wife were sending their daughters to dancing school, the couple asked to withdraw from the church. The church refused to release them—until it had tried them, humiliated them before the entire congregation, then turned them out.

The doctor's wife, in a well-written letter explaining her views to the church session, summed it up: "I thank God my life is in His hands, not yours. . . . You say you have judged my case by the Bible. . . . The Bible has been the most abused book in the world. . . . It is made to prove anything its interpreters want."

Politics and Pistols
on the Frontier

Tennessee's first governor, John Sevier, stood facing a future president, both with pistols drawn and fire in their eyes. It was early on a Sunday morning in October 1803 on a country road near Kingston. A seven-year feud between Sevier and Andrew Jackson had boiled to a climax.

Jackson had charged Sevier with a massive land fraud in North Carolina. Sevier branded the charges as lies, and Tennessee voters had taken the matter so lightly that they elected Sevier to a fourth term as governor. But the day after Sevier was inaugurated, on September 23, 1803, in Knoxville, the state legislature appointed a committee to investigate the land fraud charges. Sevier, fifty-eight years old and seasoned in politics and war, blazed with anger.

The investigation had been going on little more than a week, when he met one of the committee members, Colonel William Martin of Sumner County, on a Knoxville street. "Sevier berated Martin," one witness said, and soon Martin's friend, Andrew Jackson, appeared on the street. Jackson, thirty-five years old and a judge on Tennessee's superior court, was in Knoxville to preside over the court. He was presumably on the way from the courthouse to his hotel room when he encountered Sevier and Martin.

"Sevier shouted that all his enemies were 'damned cowards and dare not meet him,' " Carl S. Driver wrote in his biography, *John Sevier*.

"Jackson demanded an explanation. James Sevier, son of the governor, raised a large stone in his hand and ordered Jackson to stand off. The judge told Sevier if he had any malice against him, a modest hint to meet him behind a grove would be sufficient. The governor dared the judge to open combat in the street. The governor was armed with a cutlass, and the judge, with a sword-cane, was just recovering from a severe illness. Colonel Martin took Judge Jackson by the arm and they walked toward their lodging, and the governor followed, making use of every insulting and abusive expression."

When Jackson said he had performed some services for the state, Sevier dragged out the favorite insult to Jackson. "Service?" Sevier said. "I know of no great service you have rendered the country except taking a trip to Natchez with another man's wife."

"Great God!" Jackson answered. "Do you mention her sacred name?" referring to the mix-up over the date of his wife's divorce from her former husband.

Jackson next day had a note delivered to Sevier, challenging him to a duel. "The ungentlemanly expressions and gasconading conduct of yourself was in true character of yourself, and unmasked you to the world, and plainly shows that they were the ebulitions of a base mind, goaded with stubborn proofs of fraud, and flowing from a source devoid of every refined sentiment or delicate sensation," Jackson wrote Sevier. "But Sir, the voice of the people has made you a Governor, this alone makes you worthy of my notice, or the notice of any Gentleman. For the office, I have respect, and as such only I can deign to notice you. . . ."

Sevier answered Jackson in mocking tones. He said he would meet Jackson anywhere outside Tennessee, since it was unlawful to fight a duel inside the state. Jackson answered immediately: name the place, he said, and make it "before 4 o'clock this afternoon or I will publish you as a coward and a poltroon."

But Sevier did not answer. For six days nothing happened.

Jackson wrote Sevier again and told him to name the time and place he would meet him. Again Sevier answered that he could not fight in Tennessee.

"I have some regard to the laws of the state over which I have the honor to preside," Sevier announced, "though you, a judge, appear to have none. It is to be hoped, that if by any strange and unexpected event, you should ever be metamorphosed into an upright and virtuous judge, you will feel the propriety of being governed and guided by the laws of the state you are sacredly bound to obey and regard."

Letters defending Sevier began appearing in the state's newspapers (signed "A citizen of Knox County," one of the letters is said to have been written by Sevier himself). One letter, boasting of Sevier's fifteen children, implied that Jackson, being childless, had little to lose in a duel.

On October 11, Sevier refused to open another challenging letter that Jackson had delivered to him. Three days later Sevier left Knoxville on "Indian business" and stopped overnight at a house near Kingston. The next morning, on Sunday, October 16, 1803, (less than three weeks after he had been inaugurated governor), Sevier and the three men accompanying him got an early start. Before they stopped for breakfast, they encountered Jackson on the dusty road. The various accounts of the scene that followed show it to be as comic as a rollicking Western.

Sevier's son Washington was riding alongside him. Riding in front of them were their friends, Andrew Greer and John Hunter. Jackson stopped to talk with Greer, while Van Dyke rode on to deliver a note to Sevier. Sevier refused to accept the note. At that, Greer said, Jackson threw his umbrella to the ground, drew one of his pistols, dismounted, drew the other pistol, and advanced toward Sevier. Greer "looked around and saw the governor off his horse with his pistols in his hands, advancing toward Jackson."

They stood twenty paces apart, "hurling abusive language

at each other." Governor Sevier dared Jackson to "fire away," but after a "little parley," they returned their pistols to their holsters. Jackson swore he would "cane" Sevier, and, at that, Sevier's friends said, the latter's horse was so frightened that he ran away, carrying Sevier's pistols. The trick, Jackson's friends said, was for Sevier to rid himself of arms since Jackson would not shoot an unarmed man.

"Thereupon Jackson threw down his pistol and advanced toward Sevier," Sevier's friends reported. Sevier dodged behind a tree and abused Jackson for attacking an unarmed man. Sevier's son drew a pistol and covered Jackson, and Dr. Van Dyke "threatened young Sevier in the same manner." At last Dr. Van Dyke "prevailed on General Jackson to desist, finding that General Sevier would not defend himself."

Sevier had his account of the incident published in the newspapers. He called it the "Kingston attempt to assassinate" and reminded voters that he had more important things to think about than a private feud—building a road to Georgia, for instance.

Privately, however, Sevier suffered from the affair, and he wrote an old friend, James Robertson, a few weeks later: "I make no doubt but you have heard many ill-natured things respecting me . . . of my being a rogue, a coward and a thousand other things. . . . If Jackson has any objections against me respecting land, he might have had as much and perhaps a great deal more against some nearer home. . . . I am sorry I am bound to view him as one of the most abandoned rascals in principle my eyes ever beheld."

Sevier's troubles with Jackson had begun in 1796, the year that Tennessee became a state. Jackson, Tennessee's first congressman, was twenty-nine years old then and on his way to Philadelphia to take his seat in the House of Representatives when he heard of Sevier's alleged part in land grant frauds in North Carolina. Jackson reported the alleged frauds to the governor of North Carolina, and investigations there brought about the arrest and conviction of the public official accused of accepting bribes from Sevier.

When Jackson returned from Philadelphia to Nashville in the spring of 1797, he learned that Sevier had fought back with angry letters about him. "But sir, behold my surprise when I returned," Jackson wrote Sevier on May 8, 1797, "and found that you had wrote a letter to Gen. James Robertson and another to Mr. Joel Lewis, in which you had made use of the following language respecting me, 'that you did not regard the scurrilous expression of a poor pitiful pettyfogging lawyer, and you treated them with contempt.' These sir, are expressions that my feelings are not accustomed to, and which . . . Sir, I will not tamely submit to. . . . This conduct requires an explanation and the injury done my private character and feelings require redress. . . . "

Sevier, whose home was in Knoxville, was in Nashville at the time, and he answered immediately, reminding Jackson of attacks he had made on him. Jackson wrote to Sevier on May 10, 1797:

I was neither your political foe nor private enemy, nor am I yet inclined to be so. But I feel the sweetness and necessity of protecting my feelings and reputation whenever they are maliciously injured. . . . I now remark to you that I think you had no malicious design to injure my reputation, and that your letters proceeded from the warmth of the moment. . . . It will give me pleasure to converse with you personally on this subject, in the presence of such of our friends as may be agreeable to you and myself to name. . . . Be pleased therefore to state some convenient place and time in Nashville where I can see you. . . .

But Sevier did not appear at the appointed place and time, and Jackson finally decided to drop the matter for the time being. Jackson had been elected to the U.S. Senate in 1797, but resigned in a few months to return to Nashville. Almost indifferently he accepted appointment as judge on Tennessee's superior court.

Meantime Sevier had been elected governor three times, and, according to state law, could not succeed himself again. It was then, in 1801, that Archibald Roane, Jackson's good friend since the beginning of their law practice in North Carolina, succeeded Sevier as governor.

Roane had been in office only a few months when a vacancy for a much coveted job occurred: major general of Tennessee's militia. Election to this top post in the state's military force came by vote of commissioned officers. Sevier and Jackson got the same number of votes, and Governor Roane had to break the tie. Roane had to choose between the fifty-seven-year-old Sevier, veteran Indian fighter who had already served as brigadier-general in the militia, and thirty-five-year-old Jackson, whose only military experience consisted of boyhood skirmishes with the British during the Revolutionary War

To half-French Sevier, who boasted he had fought in thirty-five battles and never lost one, Jackson was a young whippersnapper of a lawyer who was trying to push to the front too fast. It galled him that Jackson, practically untried in combat, would compete with him for the state's top military honor.

On February 16, 1802, the day that Governor Roane had to make the decision, Jackson made available to him the record of Sevier's transactions in the North Carolina land grants. Roane voted for Jackson. Sevier never forgot the sting of that defeat.

He set to work to show Jackson his political power in the state. Sevier announced he would run against Roane for the governorship. From then on, it was Sevier and his allies against the political alliance of Roane and Jackson.

The biggest gun that Roane had to fire was the matter of Sevier's land deals. Included in the damaging evidence was a letter Sevier had written on November 11, 1795, to James

Glasgow, North Carolina official who had cooperated with him in the transactions. Andrew Jackson then and historians since have interpreted certain statements in that letter as offers of bribes to Glasgow for helping Sevier get title to land not legally his. Glasgow was charged with making it possible for Sevier to steal 57,160 acres from the state, and accepting 1,920 acres as payoff for the deal.

"I am highly sensible of your goodness and friendship in executing my business at your office, in the manner and form which I took the liberty to request," Sevier's letter read in part. "I have instructed Mr. Gordon to furnish unto you a plat of the amount of three 640 acres, which I considered myself indebted to you. . . . "

Sevier, in answer to Jackson's charges of bribery, said the land he offered Glasgow was simply payment for his services, for issuing warrants to two gigantic plots of land. But the usual fee for issuing two warrants would have been one dollar, and Sevier had given land valued at not less than $960.

The legislature's investigating committee reported that the official entry book covering the date of Sevier's transactions (all made on September 16, 1779) had disappeared, and the lost record book was replaced by a book said to be in Sevier's own handwriting. The committee also reported that they were "of the opinion that warrants to the amount of 105,600 acres of land have been fraudulently obtained by John Sevier from Landon Carter (who acted as entry taker) . . . and grants surreptitiously obtained from the Secretary of North Carolina, to wit, James Glasgow, by said Sevier, on said fraudulent warrants, to the amount of 46,060 acres. . . . " It turned out later that some sixty other people had title to land that Sevier claimed.

When Governor Roane brought up the Sevier land scandal during the 1803 campaign, Sevier's friends fought back by accusing Roane of having pardoned a "young man convicted of murder, because he was the son of a general and of a rich man." Jackson, coming hotly to Roane's defense, said the charge was a lie. He, Judge Jackson, had presided at the trial, which was conducted "fairly and agreeably to the rules of law." The young man was "acquitted by a respectable and impartial jury," and the governor was in no way involved in the case.

Roane, a man of dignity and courtesy, had no taste for a mud-slinging race. He campaigned for reelection on his record as governor, as soldier in the American Revolution, as attorney general in one district of Tennessee before it became a state, as a petitioner to North Carolina to give up the land that became Tennessee, and as one who had helped draw up Tennessee's constitution.

But Roane's friend Jackson was relentless in publicizing Sevier's questionable record. Jackson knew that it would be his political prestige, not Roane's, that would be tested on election day. And Sevier's victory over Roane—not only on that election day in 1803, but also for a fifth term as governor in 1805 and a sixth term in 1807—was a severe jolt to Jackson's political hopes.

Sevier had enough political power in the legislature of 1803 to get the damning report by the investigating committee watered down to a harmless document. Sevier was never impeached or brought to trial for his alleged land frauds. He was, after his six terms as governor, elected congressman and held that post when he died in September 1815.

That was eight months after Jackson, the man Sevier had called the "poor pitiful pettyfogging lawyer," had become a national hero in his victory over the British at New Orleans. It was that victory that helped sweep Jackson into the White House thirteen years later.

Now statues of Jackson and Sevier, who once drew pistols on each other, stand with noble mien in our nation's Capitol— paired at last to represent Tennessee as two of her great men.

William Blount, First Impeachment in the Senate

Tennessee's first senator, William Blount, had the bitter distinction of being the first member of the United States Senate to be removed from his seat. The overtones of international intrigue give it current fascination. For Blount, to put it bluntly, was framed.

He had been in the Senate only one year when he was voted out, twenty-five to one, by his fellow lawmakers. It was 1797, so soon after the American Revolution that United States citizens were still suspicious of Britain. Britain, it was said, was using Blount, through his skill with the Indians, to incite them to aid Britain in her attempt to take Florida and parts of Louisiana away from Spain.

When the plot was discovered, Spain demanded reprisals. The United States government, afraid of open warfare with Spain, decided to make Blount (pronounced Blunt) the scapegoat in an embarrassing situation. President John Adams appeased Spain by having the Senate vote Blount out.

It was a shocking procedure, even in those uneven days when the new government was still feeling its way toward proper conduct of its affairs. It was not until a year and a half later, in January 1799, that Congress got around to the "hearings"—and then failed to take action because they found they had no jurisdiction.

Blount died the following year, on March 21, 1800, without ever having his name officially cleared of the "smear." Death came a few days before his fifty-first birthday, closing a unique career in Tennessee history.

He was a man of excellent family, excellent education and tremendous ambition. Ironically, one of his great goals had been to get into the United States Senate, where he sat barely six months. His whole career had been pointed in that direction.

A native of North Carolina, he fought in the Revolutionary War and was delegate to the Convention of 1787 that wrote the United States Constitution. "Mr. Blount is a character strongly marked for integrity and honor," a fellow delegate to the convention wrote at that time. "He is no speaker, nor does he possess one of those talents that make men shine —he is plain, honest and sincere."

He signed the Constitution, and he was elected to the North Carolina state legislature six times. But he failed to get the legislature to elect him to the United States Senate.

That was before North Carolina gave up its western lands that later became Tennessee. Blount looked across the mountains, where he had made treaties with the Indians as representative of North Carolina. By 1789, North Carolina had given up claim to the land, and by 1790 President George Washington appointed Blount territorial governor of Tennessee.

Automatically Blount became superintendent of Indian Affairs for the Southern Department, and out of his successful dealings with the Indians came his usefulness in the disastrous plot.

It was a difficult job—reconciling the settlers' hostility toward Indians with the federal government's attempt to deal peaceably with them. Blount managed no small feat when he kept the goodwill of all sides.

By the time the territory qualified for statehood, Blount was well aware of the federal government's distrust of southern states. The New England-dominated government feared that too many southern states in the Union would shift the power southward, would give the "Democratick" party the upper hand.

From the first, Virginia had taken such a lead in national affairs, had furnished so many powerful statesmen, including Washington and Jefferson, that northern politicians frowned on more of the same kind of competition. Another southern state meant more votes for the "Democratick" party. Conservative President Adams and his right-hand man, Alexander Hamilton, wanted none of that.

But from the same Knoxville home where he had signed Indian treaties, Territorial Governor Blount set the machinery in motion for turning the territory into the state of Tennessee. It was largely through his experience in government affairs that the new state was created, and Tennessee was admitted to the Union on June 1, 1796.

On the following August 3, the new state's legislature elected Blount to the United States Senate. In the following December, he arrived at the national Capitol in Philadelphia to be sworn into the Senate. The city was full of rumors of what Spain was going to do to blockade our southern ports from trade, and rumors of what Britain's fleet would be willing to do to prevent that.

The secret scheme of President Adams and his advisor, Hamilton, and Secretary of State Timothy Pickering was to set the Indians of Florida and Louisiana against Spanish rulers. In that way, they could be most helpful to the invading British fleet, and, indirectly, to the United States. But Adams had fought hard during his campaign for the presidency to prove that he was not pro-British, as his opponents had accused him of being. He dared not work with the British openly, but his secretary of state worked closely with the British minister, Robert Liston, to bring the scheme about.

When Blount arrived in Philadelphia, he was already established as an important negotiator with the Indians of Tennessee and adjoining areas. He was sought out as a valuable participant in the scheme—his role being to arouse Tennessee

Indians to influence Florida Indians against Spain, "at the proper time."

Blount justified his action by saying it was essential to Tennessee's commerce to keep the Mississippi River open to traffic from New Orleans. Tennessee's constitution contained an article to that purpose: "That an equal participation in the free navigation of the Mississippi River is one of the inherent rights of the citizens of this State, it cannot, therefore, be ceded to any prince, potentate, power or person or persons whatsoever."

To get things moving among the Tennessee Indians, Blount wrote a letter to James Carey, his interpreter among Indians in the Knoxville area. The letter, dated April 21, 1797, and written in Philadelphia, was the damning evidence that ended Blount's career, but it was so cautiously worded that the strongest sentence in it simply called on Carey to "keep things in proper frame for action in case it should be attempted. You must take care in whatever you say . . . not to let the plan be discovered by Hawkins, Dinsmore, Dyers or any other persons in the interest of the United States nor Spain," Blount cautioned Carey. "If I attempt this plan, I shall expect to have you and all my Indian country and Indian friends with me, but you . . . are not to say anything . . . until you again hear from me. . . . When you have read this letter over three times, then burn it."

But Carey did not burn the letter, and he confessed that he got drunk a few days later and showed it to a Knoxvillian working for the Spanish minister to the United States. There was a "terrible to-do about it at Knoxville," and Blount wrote from Philadelphia that "it makes a damnable fuss here."

The Spanish minister to the United States wrote an insolent letter to President Adams, giving him and his advisors a mighty scare about possible exposure of their own part in the affair. Adams knew that it would end his political career if evidence of his collusion with Britain became known. He decided to make Blount the scapegoat.

Actually Blount was a small part of the plan, and British Minister Liston hurriedly advised Adams and Secretary of State Pickering to ignore the whole thing. But Adams saw a fine opportunity for damaging the "Democratick party" by pretending that all of the blame was Blount's. Accordingly he ordered the letter to be read to both houses of Congress, and he publicly professed great shock at such goings-on. He instigated plans for impeachment, and the word was passed along to the Senate to vote Blount out. The Adams-controlled Senate followed orders, and only five days after the Blount letter was exposed, they ousted him by a vote of twenty-five to one. That was July 8, 1797; impeachment proceedings in the House began at once.

Even with the guilt pinned on Blount, however, the British minister was still terrified at the public disclosure of the scheme. He dashed off notes to his government in Britain outlining the political reasons behind President Adams's embarrassing action. Liston wrote that our government had determined to expose the letter because "Blount, a member of the senate from Tennessee, a man of an active and turbulent character. . .was unfriendly to the present administration."

On the very day that Blount was voted out of the Senate, Liston reported to his government that "the administration no doubt thought that the disgrace of a man who had been vehemently opposed to the measures of the administration would have some effect in humbling and weakening the Democratick party in general. . . . Mr. Adams therefore resolved to communicate the business. . .to the two houses of congress and to leave them to take such measures. . .as they might think expedient."

The Britisher made it clear that Adams and his cabinet would take pains to cover up Britain's blame in the scheme. "The Secretary of State gave me an opportunity to exculpate myself and the British government of any degree of blame in this business. . . . The fact is . . .I believe the United

States . . .would have been glad to see this carried into execution."

The British minister, in the same letter, emphasized the insignificance of Blount's role in the scheme that Adams, Hamilton, Pickering, and the British had concocted. "It is singular enough that Governor Blount is a man whom I have never seen and with whom I have had no communication either direct or indirect," Liston wrote. "I did not even know till I read his letter that he was one of the persons concerned in the plan. Mr. Chisholm [a go-between used by Liston] used to mention him as a man of weight and influence in the back country whom it would be essential to gain, but he seemed to doubt the possibility of securing him." So, by their own admission, the instigators of the plot had not even been sure that Blount would join them.

But Blount stood so high in the opinion of Tennesseans that he was elected to the state senate when he returned home from Philadelphia, and he was made Speaker. He did not bother to go back to Philadelphia for the Senate impeachment proceedings that began in January 1779, and the lawyers who represented him put little vigor into the project. By that time, the president was openly "calling on all Americans to draw the sword on the side of England." Apparently weary of the whole business, the Senate decided on Friday, February 11, 1799, that they had no jurisdiction over the Blount case and that they "ought not to hold court of the said impeachment and the said impeachment is dismissed."

A few years later our armies had removed all foreign governments from Florida and Louisiana, and Andrew Jackson became a national hero for his part in it. But Blount died in 1800 without having his name cleared of the doubtful distinction of being the first senator removed from office.

He Killed Tecumseh

Richard Mentor Johnson, who was the first of the nation's three vice-presidents named Johnson, startled travelers at his Kentucky inn near Lexington in 1839.

There was no doubt about the lavish hospitality of this rugged Indian fighter whom Andrew Jackson had backed for the vice-presidency under President Martin Van Buren. But for the vice-president, even while he held that office, to be "tavern-keeping, even giving his personal superintendence to the chicken and egg purchasing and watermelon selling department" was a shock.

He made no excuses about his Negro mistress who helped him run the place, or about the two daughters who were his by another mulatto. He had even tried to get the girls accepted in Kentucky society and had taken them on a trip with him to New York. Even the red vest that became his "trademark" at Washington dinner parties paled by comparison.

Politicians—as much as they revered the "gallant colonel" who had killed the fearless Tecumseh in the war of 1812— knew he would be an easy target for the opposition once word of his "youthful indiscretion" spread.

"I stopped yesterday evening at Col. Johnson's watering establishment and remained today," one contemptuous traveler wrote from Johnson's resort hotel at White Sulphur Springs, Kentucky, in August 1839. "The old gentleman seems to enjoy the business of *Tavern-Keeping* as well as any host I ever stopped with, and is as bustling a *land lord* as the most fastidious traveller could wish. The example of Cin-

85

cinnatus laying down his public honors and returning to his plough should no longer be quoted as worthy of imitation, when the Vice President of these United States, with all his civic and military honors clustering around his time honored brow, is, or seems to be so happy in the inglorious pursuit of tavern keeping."

For years people had been gossiping about Julia Chinn, the mulatto woman who some said had been his wife. Certainly she was his mistress for many years and was the mother of his two daughters, Adaline and Imogene. Julia, whom Johnson had inherited as a slave from his father's estate, had been trained and brought up in the household as a servant of Johnson's proud and well-educated mother. In the years that Johnson was in Washington as congressman and senator, Julia ran his Kentucky home and brought up their children.

Johnson was devoted to the girls, and saw to it that they had private tutoring from the best teacher available. His big brick home at Blue Springs was famed for its hospitality, and he saw to it that his daughters sat at the table with distinguished guests, including Lafayette, the French hero who made his triumphal tour of the country in 1824. Johnson, a national hero himself at the moment, gave one of the state dinners that Kentucky offered the Frenchman, and Lafayette spent the night in Johnson's home. Presidents Jackson, Van Buren, and Monroe were overnight guests. Politicians, judges, scholars, and ministers flocked to his table when he was home from Washington.

It was an atmosphere that Johnson had known all his life. His father, Robert, had been one of those who helped draw up the constitution for Kentucky when that state was sliced off the western end of Virginia. As judge, churchman, land owner, he was one of the powers in the state. Richard's mother—famed for her bravery in an Indian raid and her piety and devotion to learning all her life—was a descendant of the Lees of Virginia. Her fifth child, Richard, was born during an Indian raid in 1780, soon after she and her husband arrived at the frontier settlement called Beargrass (site of Louisville today). Richard, with a tremendous thirst for learning, received four years of rigid schooling in Latin and grammar before he studied law. He began practicing law when he was nineteen, and found himself swamped with work, defending "indigent but honest citizens" caught in the expensive business of trying to unscramble conflicting land claims.

"Championing the cause of the poor against the rich" did not make money for Richard Johnson, but it won him friendships that swept him into the state legislature before he was old enough to serve. The people were so eager to have him as their representative that "no questions of age were asked," and he was elected "almost by acclamation." He was the first native Kentuckian to go to that state's legislature, or to the United States Congress, or to the vice-presidency. He was twenty-six years old when he was elected to Congress, where he served from 1807 to 1819. He voted for declaration of war against Great Britain, and took time away from congressional duties to go home and form his own regiment of mounted riflemen. Among the volunteers in his regiment were his brother James and James's sons, aged fifteen and seventeen, who helped bring about one of the dramatic victories of the War of 1812.

It was in the fall of 1813, on the River Thames near the Canadian border, that Johnson fought the bloody battle. He learned from a captured soldier that the British had eight hundred men along the river bank just in front of them. Indians were fighting for the British, and there were fifteen hundred of them hidden in the tall grass and heavy underbrush of the swampland just to the right of the British line.

The plan was for Richard's brother, James, to attack the British at the same moment that Richard attacked the Indians. It worked. James's men diverted one flank of the British line, then rode straight through the astonished British ranks to wheel and attack them from the rear. The terrified British "surrendered as fast as they could throw down their guns," and that part of the battle was over in five minutes.

Meanwhile, Richard led twenty men "a few rods in front of the main body" of his army to draw the first fire of the Indians. He found the marshy ground littered with fallen trees, impossible for mounted attack. Nineteen of the twenty men fell in the first volley fired by the Indians, and Johnson ordered his regiment to dismount. He alone stayed on his horse, though both he and his animal were wounded.

As the Indians leaped out of the grass, they took their cue from their chief, who turned out to be the famous Tecumseh. As Johnson's men attacked the Indians hand to hand, he saw his chance for a surprise attack on the chief. But just before he reached him, the wounded horse stumbled. Tecumseh turned and leveled his rifle at Johnson; the bullet shattered his hip and thigh.

The Indian "grinned horribly a ghastly smile," and "with a fierce look of malicious pleasure" raised his tomahawk. Johnson emptied his pistol in the breast of the chief, who fell dead on the spot. The Indians near him, "filled with consternation . . . raised a horrid yell and instantly fled."

The battle was soon over. The victory was the shot in the arm the nation needed in a period of blackest despair. And Johnson's victory over Tecumseh, "the most courageous, most hostile, most skillful, and most terrific savage foe that America ever had," built a special aura around the Kentuckian.

Poems and plays were written about him and his Kentucky constituents held patriotic rallies in his honor. Later, when he was considered for the presidency and elected vice-president, the campaign chant began: "Rumpsey, Dumpsey, Colonel Johnson killed Tecumseh!"

But he paid for that victory with wounds that plagued him the rest of his life. Wounded five times, the thirty-three-year-old Johnson fell off his horse just after he killed Tecumseh and was taken to Detroit for surgery. After nine days of treatment there, he was placed in a bed improvised in a carriage for a "distressing journey" to his Kentucky home. He reached there in November 1813, and by January, still in pain, "set out for Washington, a journey of 600 miles, with none but a faithful servant to accompany him, on his way back to congress."

Congress gave the hobbling soldier a hero's welcome. He was hard at work the following August when the British burned the Capitol and was chairman of a committee appointed to investigate the laxity of certain government officials in allowing the city to be taken. Later he was chairman of the committee appointed to investigate Andrew Jackson's campaign against the Seminoles in Florida. He was the only member of that committee who reported that Jackson had acted legally. Henry Clay prepared the majority report, condemning Jackson for his action. Johnson insisted on presenting his minority report. When the two Kentucky orators had presented their opposite views, Congress voted to accept Johnson's report. Jackson never forgot Johnson's role in the controversy.

Johnson retired from Congress in 1819 and returned to Kentucky. His neighbors promptly elected him to the state legislature, which just as promptly elected him to the United States Senate. (All senators were elected by state legislatures at that time.) Among other things, Johnson fought to abolish imprisonment for debts. His own heavy debts gave him thorough understanding of the plight of frontiersmen who risked all in land and business ventures, and often lost.

His father had died a wealthy man, leaving land and slaves to all of his children, and Richard Johnson and his brothers had many business ventures—operating farms, country stores, printing offices, newspapers, health resorts. Richard never hesitated about going on his brothers' notes or they on his, and creditors "hounded" him incessantly. The four Johnson brothers put up such a solid front and succeeded in so many ventures (three of them were congressmen, two senators, two judges) that political enemies accused them of trying to set up a "Johnson dynasty."

Richard Johnson never married (unless, as some newspapers reported, he married the first of his mulatto mistresses). In his thirty-six years in Washington life, he never established a home of his own except for the four years he was vice-president. The rest of the time he had an apartment in the home of a friend, and dined often at the White House or at the homes of cabinet members.

Matchmakers tried to marry their daughters to him, even as he gave his blessings to his two daughters in their marriage to white men. He deeded a farm and a home and other property to each daughter and her husband and settled other property on his one grandson.

In Congress he devoted much effort to getting pensions for old soldiers. Between sessions of Congress, when he was back in Kentucky, his home was cluttered with old soldiers needing a free meal or a night's lodging. And he made a point of placing rich man, poor man, scholar, and tramp side by side at his table.

Like his parents, who had been among the founders of the little Baptist church near their home, he pushed mission work among the Indians, and he worked for special schools to educate them. In fact, he gained some renown from the school for Choctaw boys that he established practically in the yard of his own home.

In Washington, ladies spoke of his "great gentleness," and men of his generosity and diplomacy. When Jackson's cabinet was split by the Peggy Eaton affair (cabinet member John H. Eaton had married a taverner's daughter, and other cabinet members' wives would not attend functions where Peggy was invited), Johnson worked to bring peace again.

Jackson backed Johnson in his candidacy for vice-president

on the ticket with Van Buren in 1836. There were four candidates for vice-president. Johnson, though he had the largest
number of electoral votes, did not have the majority. The
election was thrown into the Senate, where the vote was for
Johnson thirty-three to sixteen. He was the only vice-president
in our history elected by the Senate. Johnson was inaugurated
on March 4, 1837, and by the end of his term was considered
for the presidency.

His first mistress, Julia Chinn, had died in a cholera epidemic in 1833, and one of his daughters, Adaline (married to
a Mr. Scott), died three years later. People continued to spread
the story of his mulatto mistresses who succeeded Julia, and
even his old friend Jackson considered Johnson, as the vice-
presidential candidate, a "dead weight" around Van Buren's
neck in the campaign of 1840. They were defeated, and after
their successors were sworn into office on March 4, 1841,
Johnson left Washington, never to return.

In the nine years left to him, he made another try for
president and vice-president, but the younger generation of
voters was no longer stirred by the word "Tecumseh." When
the old campaigner decided to run for the state legislature in
1850, nobody would run against him. The seventy-year-old
warrior was being "talked up" for governor when he died of a
stroke at 4:00 A.M. on November 19, 1850, in his Frankfort,
Kentucky, lodging place.

The "gallant colonel" who had boasted that he was
"born in a canebrake and cradled in a sap trough" had thrilled a
nation and shocked a society as much as any public figure.
But—unlike those other two vice-presidents named Johnson—
he never made it to the White House. His fame vanished with
his life.

The White-Hot
Blaze of Courage

Entering the ruins of the Alamo in San Antonio, Texas, today, where courage leaped to a white-hot blaze one March day in 1836, is an exercise in contrasts.

No view of open land there now. No sweep of Texas plains. Thick-walled and quiet as a tomb, in the midst of downtown San Antonio, the once fiery fortress drowses. Tall office buildings stare down on the ancient stone walls where all of the 183 defenders died. In the cold stone barracks, once priests' quarters in the old Spanish mission, they had stacked enemy bodies to build human barricades. When their ammunition was gone, they had swung their guns like clubs and fought with knives in a grisly climax to the thirteen-day siege.

There were more fighting men there from Tennessee— thirty-four in all—than from any other state, and none played more dramatic roles than these Tennesseans. Leading them was David Crockett, frontier hero, who was given the toughest spot at the fortress to defend. There, just outside the chapel door, he died—his "Tennessee boys" around him, his coonskin cap beside him.

There was Tennessee-born Jim Bowie, inventor of the Bowie knife, who had "raised hell from Tennessee to Texas" before he gathered some thirty men to go to the defense of the Alamo. Some say he died with his Bowie knife in his hand.

There was Almeron Dickinson, a Tennessee blacksmith in charge of artillery at the Alamo. He had eloped with the maid of honor on the way to his own wedding in Bolivar, Tennessee, and moved on to Texas.

There was Dickinson's impetuous wife, Susannah, a spunky girl from Bolivar, who played one of the strangest roles in the whole saga of the Alamo. She, with their infant daughter, was the only American woman within the walls during the battle. Spared because she was a woman, she lived to tell the world what happened there.

There was Albert Martin, a hard-riding Tennessean chosen to slip out of the Alamo, through the Mexican lines, during the battle to tell Texas of Santa Anna's attack. He brought thirty-two more men back to help in the defense.

After Tennessee, with 34 men at the Alamo, came Kentucky, with 14; and Virginia and Pennsylvania with 11 each. The rest of the 183 came from South Carolina, New York, Missouri; Mississippi, Massachusetts, Louisiana and Georgia; Alabama, Maryland, North Carolina, Ohio and Arkansas; New Jersey, Illinois; Ireland, England, Scotland, Germany, Wales and Denmark.

None were professional soldiers; none had gone to Texas to fight. The ways that led them there were as varied as men's ambitions, romances, whims. One by one, some with a bride, some with a fiddle or a lawbook or surveyor's instruments, the Tennesseans had found their way to Texas, land of opportunity, land of wealth.

At that time Texas was part of Mexico. The excitement of this wide land, where practically free acres could be had by the thousands, had fired the imagination of two continents. For some eleven years before the Battle of the Alamo, Mexico had been coaxing settlers there with offers of tax-free land and all the privileges of a democratic government.

Saloons in New Orleans were crowded with speculators on their way to Texas to make a killing. Boats from Europe were bringing in Texas-bound men from England, Ireland,

Wales, Germany, Denmark. But most of the settlers were from the United States, and the Mexicans suddenly realized, in 1835, that there wasn't much Texas land left. Already some thirty-five thousand Americans had moved in, and the tide was growing. Suddenly the democracy turned into a dictatorship. Land contracts were broken. New restrictions hampered Americans' movement and trade. Mexico was determined to throw the Americans out. Every settler in Texas had been required to take the oath of allegiance to Mexico, and to join the Catholic Church.

Most had voted for Mexico's flamboyant president, Anthonio Lopez de Santa Anna, because he promised to uphold democracy. Instead, he turned into a tyrant—abolishing the legislature, dismissing his cabinet, so abusing his people that even today historians rate him the most hated president in Mexican history.

As his threats to Texans gained momentum, they saw no answer but revolt. In the fall of 1835, they began the clumsy process of hurriedly setting up a provisional government and gathering volunteers to protect their land. They would either force Santa Anna to restore their rights, or they would set up a new country: the Republic of Texas.

Immediately destiny drew a bead on the Alamo. In that three-acre fortress, and in the old Spanish town of San Antonio just across the river, was a garrison of Mexican troops commanded by Santa Anna's own brother-in-law, General Cos. The Americans decided to drive them out. In December 1835, the tiny army of 240 Texans, fighting from house to house for five days, dislodged Cos's troops from the town. The general decided to surrender. The Texans let him and his soilders go home to Mexico. Santa Anna was furious. At that very moment, he was drilling his army of five thousand men, preparing them for the march north from Mexico City to crush the Texas rebellion. He, the luxury-loving president of Mexico, would ride at the head of the army that would recapture the Alamo.

The Texans were disorganized and anything but ready for war. Nobody was quite sure who was in charge or what to do next. They could not agree on whether to try to hold the Alamo against the approaching army.

Sam Houston, in charge of the Texas army, said no. He preferred fighting on the open plain, where there was more maneuverability. Besides, the Alamo was too remote, too far from American colonies and supplies, he said. But Henry Smith, provisional governor, decided that the show-down battle with the Mexicans should be fought at the Alamo. He sent dashing young Lieutenant Colonel William Barret Travis to strengthen the fortifications and gather supplies for a long siege. The Texans were hurriedly assembling volunteers at three points: the Alamo; Gonzales, an American community about seventy miles to the east; and Goliad, about ninety-five miles southeast of the Alamo.

Houston was at Goliad when Jim Bowie stopped there in January 1836 on his way to the Alamo. Houston sent word by Bowie to Colonel Travis: he was to blow up the Alamo before the Mexicans got there.

Colonel Travis, a romantic, party-loving, twenty-six-year old South Carolina lawyer who had come west after a broken marriage, didn't like the looks of the Alamo himself. He sent word to Governor Smith that he had rather resign his commission than try to hold the Alamo.

But Smith never answered the letter, and Bowie never delivered Houston's message to Travis. Dispirited Travis, with only forty men at first, worked doggedly at trying to mount cannons atop the Alamo walls and lay in supplies for the men he hoped to have there.

Then Bowie arrived with thirty men—and the Alamo was never the same again. A swashbuckling racketeer, born at Elliott Springs, Tennessee (in an area now inside the Kentucky line), Bowie had run away from home at fourteen and made a fortune in black-market slaves (with Pirate Jean Lafitte's help), in sawmills, and in Louisiana sugar. His crooked land transactions in Arkansas had put him in trouble with the law, but had not kept him out of the legislature. His dueling knife, designed by him for more effective carving of the enemy, had made him a legend on the frontier. Then he went to Texas.

In one of the great romances of the day, he courted and married a Spanish beauty named Ursula, daughter of an influential aristocrat in San Antonio. It was, Spaniards said, one romance that never faded. When Bowie was away on Indian raids or business trips, his bride always closed her letters with the tender farewell: "Receive thou the heart of thy wife." Then disaster struck. A cholera epidemic in 1833 killed Ursula, their two infants, and Ursula's parents.

Bowie sold his Texas lands and business and went back to Mississippi to mourn. In 1835 he returned to become a colonel in the Texas rangers. Indians called him "Fighting Devil." Texans nicknamed him the "Young Lion." When he arrived at the Alamo a month before the battle began, he stayed roaring drunk most of the time.

Men in the Alamo—distrustful of young Travis's fitness to command them—voted to make Bowie, then forty years old, their commanding officer. He turned the offer down. There was a wide rift between the two men, Travis and Bowie. They finally decided on a joint command that would make an old campaigner shudder: Travis would command the regulars and Bowie the volunteers.

It was two weeks after Bowie's arrival that Davy Crockett rode into the fortress with his twelve "Tennessee boys." All of them were new arrivals in Texas. They had plans for practicing law, or medicine, or farming. They had no land there to protect yet, but they volunteered to help out at the Alamo. Crockett himself had no idea of fighting when he left

Tennessee and set out for Texas in the fall of 1835. He would make a fortune in land there, he thought.

In January 1836, little more than a month before he died at the Alamo, his first letter home was bouncy with enthusiasm for Texas.

"What I have seen of Texas, it is the garden spot of the world—good land, plenty of timber, good mill streams, good range, clear water & every opportunity of health . . . game a plenty," he wrote.

"I am in great hopes of making a fortune for myself and family, bad as has been my prospects."

But first, he had other business to take care of. "I . . . have enrolled my name as a volunteer for six months, and will set out for the Rio Grande in a few days with the volunteers of the U.S."

At fifty, Crockett was a living legend. Wherever he appeared in Texas, the crowds cheered. At Nacogdoches, a wide-open gambling town near the Louisiana border, they fired a cannon to welcome him. At the Alamo, the reception for Crockett and his "Tennessee boys" was rollicking. First an all-night fandango, with fiddles playing and Mexican girls to dance with. Then a demand that he make a speech and become their commanding officer.

Crockett, in coonskin cap and his best story-telling form, made a rousing speech, but he turned down the job of commanding the fort. He would serve under Travis, he said.

Most of the men there were in their twenties and thirties. A few were in their teens. John Camp Goodrich, of Nashville, was just nineteen. He had left his father's farm in Neely's Bend a few weeks earlier to visit an older brother in Texas, Dr. Benjamin Briggs Goodrich, at the Texas town named Washington. "Johnny had no intention of moving to Texas," Stanley F. Horn, Nashville historian and descendent of the Goodrich family, said. "But when David Crockett came along trying to get men to go to the Alamo, Johnny went. He wanted to be where the action was."

So did John M. Hays of Nashville, twenty-two-year-old son of Andrew Hays, who lived just down the road from the Goodrich farm, at Haysboro. Hays had arrived at the Alamo before Crockett got there. He was one of the men stationed there in January when the soldiers voted for their representative at the Texas constitutional convention. Hays got one vote himself.

Sterling C. Robertson was another Nashvillian at the Alamo. He had brought a group of Tennessee families to Texas the year before and settled them in a community on the Brazos River, in East Texas. He named the place Nashville in honor of his home town, and spread the word up and down the road that they had better ride across the state to help at the Alamo.

John H. Dillard of Nashville went with him. So did Joseph Bayliss, a twenty-nine-year-old bachelor from Clarksville, who had just arrived in Texas. He joined Crockett's outfit. An ex-Tennessee woman, Elizabeth Deardorf George, thought it was bad enough when her husband, James George, left her and the children at their new home in Gonzales to ride off to the Alamo. But when her nineteen-year-old brother, Henry Deardorf, insisted on going too, she was desolate.

From Columbia, Tennessee, came the Walker cousins, Asa, twenty-three, and Jacob, thirty-one. Jacob is said to have been the last to die at the Alamo. Asa, living at Washington on the Brazos, was in such a hurry to get to the fort that he borrowed his roommate's gun and overcoat and left a note of apology. "I took the responsibility of taking your overcoat and gun," he wrote to W. W. Grant, a Columbia citizen who had traveled with him to Texas. "Your gun they would have anyhow, and I might as well have it as anyone else. If I live to return, I will satisfy you for all. If I die, I leave my clothes to do the best you can with. You can sell them for something. ... The hurry of the moment and my want of means to do better are all the excuse I have to plead for fitting out at your expense. Forgive the presumption and remember your friend at heart. — A. Walker."

Few of the men at the Alamo were illiterates, or hillbillies, or thoughtless adventurers. Those who had ridden in for the fun of it rode out before the shooting began. Doctors in the crowd fitted out an upstairs room in the barracks as a hospital. Sympathetic Mexicans in San Antonio donated supplies and relayed reports of Santa Anna's approach.

Parties broke up in the middle of the night when Crockett put his fiddle down to confer with Bowie and Travis on whether the latest Mexican courier could be believed. The air was tense. There was little doubt that Santa Anna would strike here. The only question was: When would the other American volunteers arrive to help the 150 men at the Alamo?

Micajah Autry, cultivated North Carolinian who had practiced law in Jackson, Tennessee, several years before he went to Texas, had just arrived. "Texas fever" grabbed him. "I go the whole Hog in the cause of Texas," he wrote his wife in Tennessee just before he entered the Alamo. "I expect to help them gain their independence and also to form their civil government, for it is worth risking many lives for."

Then, on the morning of February 23, 1836, the men inside the Alamo heard the rumble of ox-carts. They looked over the wall and saw many Mexican families deserting their homes in San Antonio.

Travis and fellow officers raced to the tallest point around, the church tower in San Antonio's Main Plaza, and studied the horizon. Nothing. Travis told the sentry in the tower to ring the church bell if he saw anything suspicious. At 1:00 P.M., the clang of the bell brought Travis racing up the tower steps. From high above, the quaking sentry shouted: "The enemy are in view!"

And Then
There Were None

When the showdown came at the Alamo, Tennessee's men wore their courage as easily as a deerskin jacket.

Like David Crockett's cool acceptance of the toughest spot at the Alamo when the thirteen-day siege began. That was shortly after 1:00 P.M. Tuesday, February 23, 1836—three weeks before the Texans had thought the Mexicans would strike.

Two scouts galloped out to see for themselves what the sentry had spied from the church tower, highest point in San Antonio. What they saw stunned them: hundreds of uniformed Mexicans with breastplates gleaming in the sun.

Church bells pealed the alarm, and panic seized the town. At the foot of the church tower, in San Antonio's main plaza, soldiers from the Alamo had been lounging around, wearing off the effects of the all-night celebration of Washington's birthday.

Now they ran through San Antonio's streets, across the footbridge spanning the creek-size river at the edge of town, through the gates of the strong-walled Alamo four hundred yards away. On the way, some of them dashed into stores to grab bags of grain, coffee, and other food for the Alamo. They herded cattle across the shallow river and into the compound for meat for what might be a long battle. San Antonio's streets were jammed with jabbering Mexicans and bawling cows. Mexican women with small children were begging haven at the Alamo. A few Mexican men offered to fight alongside the Texans.

Lieutenant Colonel William Barret Travis, who with Jim Bowie, had charge of defense of both the Alamo and neighboring San Antonio, decided not to try to hold the town. He would do well to barricade his troops inside the thick walls of the fortress and hold off the enemy until help arrived.

The Alamo, Travis was convinced at last, was the "key to Texas." What his men did there would pave the way for freedom. Every day they fought would give other Texans more time to prepare for the next battle. Every Mexican they killed would make the next battle easier.

Tall, lean Travis, red-headed and twenty-six years old, bounded across the bridge ahead of his men. Even as the church bell tolled, he was in his headquarters inside the Alamo, dashing off notes of appeal for help from Texas forces at Goliad, ninety-five miles away. With only 150 men to fight at the Alamo, Travis sent couriers galloping off with messages to Colonel James Walker Fannin, who had 400 men at Goliad, and to the men still gathering at Gonzales, seventy miles away.

Then Travis looked up from his desk to the man in the door: Tennessee's David Crockett—hunter, politician, fighter, builder of high spirits.

"Colonel, here am I," Crockett said laconically. "Assign me to a position, and I and my 12 boys will try and defend it."

It must have been the most reassuring thing Travis heard that day. He assigned Crockett the most dangerous place in the fortress: a weak stretch of wall near the front of the chapel. Except for that spot, a three-foot-thick stone wall from nine to twelve feet tall surrounded the three-acre fortress known as the Alamo.

For some reason, there was a gap in the stone wall there. Only a picket fence filled the gap, though the Texans had been busy shoring up that fence with high earthworks. If anybody could hold that weakest spot in the fortress, Travis said, it was Crockett and his "Tennessee boys."

While the church bells were still ringing, Tennessee's Almeron Dickinson, in charge of artillery at the Alamo, galloped through the streets of San Antonio to the house where his Tennessee wife, Susannah, and their fifteen-month-old daughter were rooming. "Give me the baby!" he yelled to Susannah. "Jump on behind and ask me no questions!" Off to the Alamo they rode, and he installed them in one of the little rooms near the back of the roofless chapel. There they, with some Mexican women and children, were to live throughout most of the siege.

Tennessee-born Bowie, who had been coughing hard for several days, dashed off from San Antonio's main plaza to the home of his two sisters-in-law, sisters of his beautiful wife who had died three years before. He wanted the sisters to have the protection of the Alamo when the Mexicans captured San Antonio. They agreed to come.

By three o'clock that afternoon, Santa Anna and his men, with bands playing and flags flying, were filing into the same square in San Antonio where the Texans had been lounging two hours earlier. First thing the arrogant Santa Anna did was hang a blood-red flag from the church tower, in full view of the Alamo. Texans knew what that meant: no quarter, no surrender, no mercy. The Texans had an answer. They fired a cannon—an 18-pounder—that shook the town and notified couriers and fleeing refugees on distant roads that the battle had begun. Then, silence. Somebody started a rumor that the Mexicans, in their complex range of signals by band music, had indicated they wanted to negotiate. Bowie thought that was worth trying. He sent one of his men to deliver a note to Santa Anna. The Mexican president-general sent a scornful message back to the "rebellious foreigners": there was nothing to talk about except unconditional surrender.

In that first hour of battle, the joint command between Bowie and Travis had broken down. They had agreed to make no major decision without consulting each other. Travis was furious that Bowie had acted alone in sending the message to Santa Anna. Immediately Travis sent his own messenger: Tennessee's Albert Martin. When Martin got to the footbridge at the San Antonio river, Santa Anna's suave aide, Colonel Almonte, was waiting. For an hour they discussed the situation. But in the end Almonte told Martin that Santa Anna would see Travis to discuss only one thing: complete surrender. "I answered him with a cannon shot," Travis reported in a brief note to his commanding officer, Tennessee's Sam Houston, in Gonzales.

That night Bowie and Travis met in the headquarters room to thresh out a system for making their joint command work. Nothing but disaster could come of a divided course on their part. While they talked, the solution came. Bowie, torn by a racking cough, collapsed. One of the doctors in the fort was summoned, and orderlies carried Bowie off on a litter to a cot in a room where he could suffer alone.

Some said the illness was pneumonia (as doctors today believe it was). Some said it was typhoid. Bowie—the tough fighter, the daring leader—was so afraid he had something contagious that he did not want others to wait on him.

He turned his command over to Travis within hours of his collapse and ordered his men to give their new commander their absolute loyalty. His fever soared; he was often delirious. He was too weak to rise from his cot. But in moments of despair during the long siege, he had his men bring his cot out into the courtyard so he could rouse them to new valor.

For the men inside the fortress, it was a waiting game—waiting for help from outside, waiting for Santa Anna to strike. They kept a sharp look-out at all activities across the river in San Antonio.

It was obvious that the resplendent Santa Anna was waiting too. Hundreds of his men had died of cold, hunger, and illness on the long march north from Mexico, but he had more reinforcements on the way. Galled by an earlier defeat at this same spot, he was determined to make this a massacre.

While he waited, his men built trenches and breastworks to protect their approach to the Alamo. Closer and closer the fortifications crept toward the stone walls. But when the men with picks and shovels got within rifle range, Texans picked them off.

The second afternoon of the siege, the Texans got their first taste of Mexican cannon fire. Shells rained over the walls, but the Texans soon learned where to dodge. Not a man was hit. That night, Travis wrote a message that stirred the world from Gonzales to New Orleans to Louisville to London. Again he chose Tennessee's Albert Martin to get it through the Mexican lines and on to the far plains. "To the people of Texas & All Americans in the World" he addressed the appeal for help, and closed it with the resolute vow: "Victory or Death."

It was Martin who rode through the night and the next day, seventy miles east, to Gonzales, spreading the word of the Alamo's plight, rounding up sixty-two men to go back with him and help hold the fort. Before he got there, thirty of the men changed their minds. Only thirty-two made the daring dash through enemy lines to the gates of the Alamo, jubilantly opened for them at 3:00 A.M. Tuesday, March 1, a week after the siege began.

In that week, there had been violent changes in the weather, from muggy warm days at first to the howling norther that sent men out foraging for firewood at great risk. There had been gray drizzle that matched the men's spirits as they marked the days without word of reinforcements.

There had been a steady trickle of deserters among the friendly Mexicans who entered the Alamo to help the Americans defend it. There had been no night without the steady harassment of distant bugle calls and shouts, shots and cheering—all part of the cunning Santa Anna's psychological warfare. Still no man in the Alamo was injured.

Mexicans building fortifications during the day learned to look out for a sharpshooter in a coonskin cap who could pick off a man as far as his gun could shoot. "A tall man with flowing hair was seen firing from the same place on the parapet during the entire siege," a Mexican captain described him later.

> He wore a buckskin suit and a cap all of a pattern different from those worn by his comrades. This man would kneel or lie down behind the low parapet, rest his long gun and fire, and we all learned to keep at a good distance when he was seen to make ready to shoot. He rarely missed his mark, and when he fired he always rose to his feet and calmly loaded his gun, strangely indifferent to the shots fired at him by our men.
>
> He had a strong, resonant voice and often railed at us, but as we did not understand English we could not comprehend the import of his words further than that they were defiant. This man I later learned was known as 'Kwockey.'

Inside the fort, Crockett tried to divert the men with his music and funny stories. He with his fiddle and John Mc-Gregor with his bagpipe would stage musical "duels" to see who could make the most noise, and the men cheered them on with whistles and stomps. It baffled Santa Anna and his a-gents listening across the river.

But nobody inside the fortress long forgot their plight. Colonel Fannin, with his four hundred men at Goliad, should have been there long before. They could not guess that Fannin, wavering between the decision one day to go, and the next day not to go, had finally decided to sit tight at Goliad (where they were all later massacred by Santa Anna).

The thirty-two men who came to the Alamo with Martin on March 1, were the last—the only—reinforcements after the siege began.

Santa Anna meantime was getting new men and equipment almost daily. The men in the Alamo could hear the Mexicans in San Antonio cheering as cannon rumbled into town, and a total of twenty-four hundred soldiers gathered there. Santa Anna, all spit and polish, planned every detail of the battle: what each man would wear, what sort of tools he would carry for fastening the scaling ladders to the walls, what sort of blades he would carry for ripping the enemy apart in hand-to-hand fighting.

On the eleventh day of the siege, Friday, March 4, the first heavy pounding of the walls by the Mexican cannon began. They were trying to blast out the weak spots in the north wall of the century-old Spanish mission fort. The Texans worked through the night to shore up caved in sections.

The twelfth day, a warm Saturday, Travis called all the men out in the courtyard during a lull in the bombardment. Mrs. Dickinson, who helped with the cooking and other tasks, came out to listen. Travis told the men bluntly there was no longer any hope of help. He was determined to fight to the end, but if any man there wanted to try to escape, now was the time. Then Travis took his sword and drew a line in the dirt, separating himself from his men.

"I want every man who is determined to stay here and die with me to come across the line," Travis challenged them. "Who will be the first?" Every man there but one crossed the line—even Jim Bowie, too weak to stand.

"Boys, I an not able to go to you," Bowie called out, "but I wish some of you would be so kind as to remove my cot over there." They did, to a great burst of cheers.

Mrs. Dickinson witnessed the scene. So did Louis Rose, the one man who chose to escape. The old Frenchman had fought in wars in Europe, and he saw no point in losing his life in this one. Before the eyes of the other men, he scaled the wall, skidded in the blood of Mexican bodies as he drop-

ped on the other side, and disappeared into the darkness. It is
only because he found shelter the next night in the home of
old friends that the details of his escape are known. Rose
himself vanished from history.

That same night—the last night for the men at the Alamo—there was a deepening bond between them. They cook-
ed supper in front of the church, and Mrs. Dickinson made
tea. Travis took his prized gold ring off his finger, ran a string
through it to make a necklace for the Dickinson baby, and
placed it around her neck. He wanted her to have it for a
keepsake. He and his men worked through half the night to
repair the cannon damage in the north wall, and at 4:00 A.M.
he lay down to sleep.

Outside, Santa Anna had his armies creeping silently, by
distant roads and fields, to take up their positions encircling
the Alamo on all four sides. The ground was cold and the
scaling ladders clumsy to handle, but every Mexican lay there
in the night, tensed for the sprint to battle at dawn.

At 5:00 A.M. Santa Anna, well back of the lines and surrounded by bands, gave the signal, and buglers sounded the
shrill call to attack. Round and round the chain of bands encircling the Alamo took up the call, meshed with the wild
shouts of the rushing soldiers.

"Colonel Travis!" a Texas sentry on the wall shouted as
he raced down the ramp and into the barracks. "The Mexicans are coming!"

Travis grabbed sword, shotgun and jacket as he ran across
the courtyard and up the ramp to the cannons on the north
wall. "Come on, boys!" he shouted to his men as they sprang
to their stations. "The Mexicans are upon us and we'll give
them Hell!"

Instantly Travis's men were scrambling to their posts, firing their twenty cannons toward the rushing Mexicans, trying
to stop them before they got so close to the foot of the wall
that the cannon could not bear on them. Some Mexicans

made it over the nearest protective ditch, and suddenly they had their ladders against the walls. The Texans fired away with shotguns and rifles at the climbing men.

Travis, on the besieged north wall, shouting orders in both English and Spanish, fired his double-barreled shotgun point-blank at the men climbing toward him. At almost that same moment, a Mexican bullet hit him in the head. His gun fell among the enemy, and he fell inside the fort, rolling down the ramp to die in the first moments of the battle.

Mrs. Dickinson was huddled with her baby in a corner of the old chapel as flashes of cannon fire lighted the four-foot-thick walls like an inferno. Some of the cannon were mounted on a platform at the back of the roofless chapel (it had collapsed seventy-five years before), and the ancient building thundered with the echo.

Into that eerie light ran a sixteen-year-old boy, holding his shattered jaw, trying to say something to Mrs. Dickinson. But the jaw wouldn't work; the words wouldn't come. Shaking his head hopelessly, he rushed back to do battle.

Wave after wave of Mexicans charged the walls, only to meet a hail of fire. They would withdraw and regroup to charge from another position. No matter how many Mexicans the Texans shot, there were always more coming. Through the rain of cannon fire, the Mexicans—driven by merciless threats from the rear—rushed for the safer spot near the base of the wall. They climbed over each other's backs and shot blindly into their own ranks.

After three charges to take the walls had failed, Santa Anna ordered his fiercest reserves, the grenadiers and the blood-thirsty *Zapadores*, into action. As they charged, Santa Anna signaled his seven bands to pound out the most blood-curdling march of all Spanish military music: the savage *Dequello*, signaling merciless death and slaughter.

Then the Mexicans, who had lost their ladders in the pile of bodies, found a section of the wall that the Texans had repaired so hurriedly that they had left ends of supporting beams and were soon inside.

"Great God, Sue, the Mexicans are inside our walls!" Dickinson shouted to his wife, at the foot of the ramp where he fired the cannon. "If they spare you, save my child!"

Then Dickinson had his man turn the cannon around and start firing at Mexicans pouring into the fort. Crockett's "weak" point in the wall turned out to be a terror to the Mexicans. Not until they entered the walls from other directions did they wipe out Crockett and his men, who fought with a fury the enemy never forgot.

"He killed at least eight of our men, besides wounding several others," one Mexican officer reported. "This being observed by a lieutenant who had come in over the wall, he sprang at him (Crockett) and dealt him a deadly blow with his sword, just above the right eye, which felled him to the ground, and in an instant he was pierced by not less then 20 bayonets."

Crockett's men were too far away from the barracks to take refuge there—where Travis had planned a last stand. But when Travis's adjutant gave the command, Texans still at their posts on the walls retreated toward the barracks, shooting as they went. In those thick-walled rooms, built a century before as priests' quarters, the Texans dug in behind the breastworks they had built at the doors. There they fired at waves of Mexicans rushing across the courtyard, and crouched behind riddled bodies of Mexicans who fell among them.

At last, when the ammunition was gone and gunsmoke choked the few survivors, the Mexicans turned the cannon toward the barracks doors and blasted them open. Mexicans scrambled in to fight hand to hand with knives while Texans struck back with their empty guns. The Mexicans found Bowie propped on his cot, against the wall, his pistols and knife at his side. He had not been able to stand for almost two weeks, but the Mexicans who entered the room told later of his last burst of strength as he lunged for the enemy before they killed him.

Last to surrender their post were Dickinson and his crew, firing the cannon from the church. The Mexicans aimed one cannon at the old church doors and brought down the platform supporting the cannon inside, killing the men and filling the church with smoke.

Robert Evans, from Ireland by way of New York, remembered Travis's plans: the last man living was to set a torch to the rooms in the church where the gunpowder was stored. They would leave no Alamo for the Mexicans. But just as Evans, already wounded, raised the torch high to pitch it into the room, a Mexican bullet felled him.

The Mexicans were in a frenzy of murder. They killed children who had taken refuge there. They hacked away at the Texans already dead. Mrs. Dickinson and the Mexican women sat silently in their corners, awaiting the end. Suddenly Tennessee's Jacob Walker rushed into the small room and tried to hide in a corner. Four Mexican soldiers were close after him, and as Mrs. Dickinson fell to her knees to pray, they shot him. He was said to be the last to die. "Then they stuck their bayonets in his body and lifted him up like a farmer does a bundle of fodder on his pitchfork," Mrs. Dickinson recalled years later.

The soldiers were about to kill Mrs. Dickinson when an officer intervened and took her to Santa Anna. As she left the smoke-choked chapel and walked across the bloody courtyard where bodies lay all about her, she was somehow mercifully blinded to the horror. One thing she did notice and remember throughout her long life: David Crockett lying on the ground, near the chapel door, his coonskin cap beside him.

It was 6:30 A.M. now—one-and-a-half hours after the battle had begun. The sky was getting light. The sudden silence was unreal, shocking as the knowledge that all 183 defenders were dead. On March 6, 1836, the Alamo fell.

Santa Anna had the bodies of the defenders stripped, stacked between layers of wood, and burned in a great bonfire. Only exception was a Mexican who had fought with the Texans. His wife pleaded for a Christian burial, and it was granted.

Mrs. Dickinson did not know then that the Texans had killed at least six hundred of the eighteen hundred who attacked. She begged Santa Anna to allow her to take her baby back to her people at Gonzales. Moved perhaps by the youth of the twenty-one-year-old Susannah, he gave her a horse and promised her safe conduct. Her escorts soon deserted her, leaving her to make the seventy-mile ride across the plains with her baby as best she could. She no longer cared whether she lived or died, she said. When she at last poured out the tale of horror to Sam Houston, he wept as she talked.

The story she told fired the world with a hatred of Santa Anna and a sympathy for Texas that brought offers of help from all directions. Money and men poured in to help them establish a republic. But before either the money or the men got there, Houston and the Texans had done it themselves.

On April 21, just six weeks after the fall of the Alamo, Sam Houston and his Texans had their revenge.

At San Jacinto, on the southern border of Texas, Houston's men gave Santa Anna one of the most devastating defeats in history, and the rallying cry that spurred the Texans to battle was, "Remember the Alamo!" Tennessee's Houston had avenged the death of the thirty-four Tennesseans and all the other Texans who died within the walls that were to become a shrine to freedom.

TENNESSEANS WHO DIED AT THE ALAMO
Micajah Autry, Jackson
Joseph Bayliss, Clarksville
John Blair
Samuel B. Blair

James Bowie, Elliott Springs
Robert Campbell
David Crockett, who lived at several places, among them
   Greene, Lincoln, Lawrence, Franklin, Carroll, and Weakley
   counties.
Field Davis
Squire Daymon
William Henry Deardorf
Almeron Dickinson, Bolivar
John H. Dillard, Nashville
James L. Ewing
James Girard Garrett
James George
John Camp Goodrich
John M. Hays, Nashville
Charles M. Heiskell
William Marshall
Albert Martin
William Mills
Andrew M. Nelson, Shelbyville
Sterling C. Robertson
James M. Rose
Andrew H. Smith
Joshua G. Smith
A. Spain Summerlin
William E. Summers
William Taylor
John W. Thompson
Burke Trammel
Asa Walker, Columbia
Jacob Walker, Columbia
Joseph G. Washington

Forgotten President

Odd, they said, the way Sam Polk's son, Jim, perked up after that horrible ordeal in Kentucky.

In 1812, surgery was new, and nobody would undergo it except as a last resort. But sickly James Knox Polk, seventeen years old and doubled up in pain much of the time, had ridden horseback the 230 miles from his father's Maury County farm to Danville, Kentucky, to see the famous surgeon, Dr. Ephraim McDowell.

There was no anesthetic then, but they strapped the thin, undersized boy to a wooden table, gave him brandy, made the incision, and removed the gallstone. It was like a new life to Jim when he recovered from surgery and, months later, he headed for home on horseback. He would make that life count, the Presbyterian-born boy resolved. He would make up for his small size and weak body by doing something really impressive.

Not then did he dream of the White House, and thirty-two years later, when he became the youngest president until that time, he had no illusions about his greatness.

He was so hounded by bickering and vicious opposition through years as Speaker of the House in Washington, as governor of Tennessee, as president of the United States that, when his term was up, he wanted nothing so much as to come home to Nashville and forget about it.

As it turned out, he died three months after he came home, and practically everybody did forget about him for more than a century. But now the Polk boom is on again. In

recent years, he has taken a new place in history. Some scholars call him the "most successful" of all presidents—if he is
judged by what he accomplished in office. Some call him the
"most neglected."

Polk ranks among the ten top presidents in every list
drawn up by historians in the last twenty-five years. Only
five—Lincoln, Washington, Franklin D. Roosevelt, Wilson and
Jefferson—were ranked "great" in a poll of seventy-five distinguished historians in 1954. The six men in the next group,
the "near great," include two Tennesseans: Andrew Jackson
at the top of the list and James K. Polk close behind. Among
Polk's claims to fame was that he, more than any other man,
was responsible for pushing our nation's borders to the Pacific Ocean. And he was one of the earliest champions of the
"little man."

But at the time Jim Polk returned from surgery in Kentucky, he had no idea what he wanted to do. He had been
too ill to attend school regularly, and it was apparent to his
father and to his grandfather, Ezekiel Polk, that he would
never be strong enough to manage the vast farm land they
had amassed since they arrived from North Carolina six years
earlier.

Sam Polk helped the boy get a job in a store in Columbia,
hoping to set him up in a mercantile business of his own later. But Jim Polk hated it. He wanted to learn some profes-
sion, and his father sent him to a small academy at Zion
Church in the nearby Frierson community. That was in 1813,
when Jim Polk was eighteen. He outstripped everybody else
in school, and the next year his father sent him to a more advanced school in Murfreesboro. His "fine gray eyes" were
glued to books so constantly that his health suffered, but in
two years he was graduated as "much the most promising
young man in the school."

The twenty-year-old youth was determined to enter the
University of North Carolina. He passed the examinations in

Latin, Greek, and English, and was admitted to the sopho-more class. There he found himself. He never again doubted what he wanted to do—to go into politics—after he discover-ed his oratorical ability in university debating societies. He was not dramatic or particularly appealing. His voice was nothing special, but he dug hard for the facts and lined them up in invincible order. When he faced an audience, he was confident, self-assured.

Jim Polk graduated from the university in May 1818 at the top of his class, but he had studied so hard he was in a state of collapse, too ill to travel. Not until the following October could he make the trip to Columbia.

His father and mother, with their nine other children, had moved into town in a fine brick home on the best street in Columbia. Jim did not tarry there long; he went to Nashville to study law with Felix Grundy, leading lawyer and a politi-cal power in the state.

On a hot summer day in 1819, he heard Grundy advise another young lawyer, Francis B. Fogg, to apply for the job as clerk of the state legislature. Fogg said he didn't want the post. Polk asked Fogg if he would use his influence to help him get the position, and Fogg agreed to that.

The same year that Polk was admitted to the bar in Columbia (he told his family to call him *James* from that date on), he began his work as clerk of the legislature, meet-ing in Murfreesboro, then the capital. Polk earned his six dol-lars a day by his "careful, business-like habits." There was no question about his being reelected without opposition for the next session and two special sessions.

Between sessions, Polk built a strong law practice in Co-lumbia, but his driving interest was in the maneuvers in the legislature, in every shrewd move. "Everything here is done by management," one new member observed. "Intrigue and bargaining are at the bottom of everything."

Polk had an eye on the slow turn in national politics,

too—away from the bankers whom poor men were blaming for the financial crisis of 1819 and toward the political revolution that would sweep Andrew Jackson into the White House nine years later.

In 1822, when Polk was about to marry and thought it time he run for the state legislature, he was already turning toward the fight for the little man's rights. His opponent was an experienced and popular member of the legislature. Doggedly, methodically, Polk rode up and down the creeks of Maury County to explain his views. When the legislature met in Murfreesboro in 1823, he took his place in his first elected office. (A fellow legislator: David Crockett.)

Banking laws were the big issue, and party lines were being chiseled out by the stand a man took. Polk, then as later, was for getting banks out of the hands of the government. He fought the stifling tax laws and the evils of land speculation and caught the eye of the state's leaders, including his lifelong hero, Andrew Jackson. Polk made a point of never allying himself too closely with anyone. But he saw things as Jackson saw them, and when there was talk of Jackson's running for the presidency, Polk offered his full support.

Polk was urged to run for Congress, and he took on four strong opponents. He "lived on his horse" for six months of intensive campaigning, and won easily.

He married Sarah Childress, daughter of a wealthy Murfreesboro merchant and landowner, on New Year's Day, 1824, and Sarah, who loved beautiful clothes, sprightly conversation and the excitement of politics, was eager to join the heady Washington crowd.

But she stayed at home in Columbia, in their cottage across the street from Polk's parents during his first session, and Polk lived in a boarding house with other Tennessee congressmen in Washington. The next session, Sarah went along, and they drove their own carriage and took two servants. On the way, at Nashville, they picked up Sam Houston, who was also in Congress then.

In Washington, David Crockett, the raw-boned bear-killer, was again a fellow legislator. Tennessee, in fact, was producing a striking surge of frontier vigor on the national scene. Polk became President Jackson's right hand man in Congress. He refused to have anything to do with the gossip when one of Jackson's cabinet members, John H. Eaton, married a Washington tavern-keeper's daughter, Peggy O'Neale. Other cabinet members and congressional wives snubbed the lively Peggy, and brought on a split in the government. When Sarah Polk joined in the snubbing, her husband left her at home in Columbia one session to think matters over.

Polk was in Congress in 1832 when his old friend Sam Houston breezed into Washington, fresh out of exile among the Indians. Houston caned a congressman who had made false statements about him, and the congressman had Houston "tried" before the House. Polk was among the Tennessee congressmen who rallied to Houston's aid and gathered in his hotel room the night before the verdict to drink to a happy outcome.

Throughout his fourteen years in Congress—four of them as Speaker—Polk pressed his fight for low taxes, no tariff and cheap land. He worked doggedly to cut down the tariff inequities that New Englanders had set up to make their part of the country richer and the South poorer.

Sometimes when the ailing Polk came home to campaign between terms, he found himself a hero, worn out by the massive wining and dining. Sometimes he found the opposition so firmly entrenched that he had to fight for every vote and take to his bed at the end of the campaign.

When Polk became Speaker of the House in 1835, a bitter clique lined up against him. They regularly announced in Washington hotels their plans for harassing him the next day as he presided, and they invited crowds to come watch the show.

President Jackson warned Polk that his life was in danger.

The opposition was trying to provoke him to a duel; Polk re-fused to be baited. Cool, courteous, a skilled parliamentarian who steered the house through dizzying traps set for him, Speaker Polk won the respect of his stubbornest opposition.

New Englanders, "shaking with wrath" over proposed changes in tariff laws, decided to get even with Southern states by making an issue of slavery. Throughout a three-month fight in 1836, the New Englanders sought to drive a wedge between Northerner and Southerner, between liberal Southerner and conservative Southerner, and Polk tried to hold a scrupulously fair line as he presided over the debates.

After President Jackson left office at the end of two terms, Polk was equally valuable to President Van Buren. And Van Buren, as president, visited the Polks in Columbia. In Washington, while Polk was Speaker of the House, he and Sarah entertained handsomely in their fashionable home. They splurged on a fine new coach that had Venetian blinds at the windows and champagne-colored upholstery.

Polk became a serious contender for the vice-presidency in 1836, but a financial crash had almost wrecked Jackson's party in Tennessee, and Polk was called home to run for gov-ernor and help re-build the party. His victory in Tennessee against tremendous obstacles was a matter of national signifi-cance, and political leaders began to look on him as a man who could do the impossible. But national leaders of the Whigs, the opposition party, concentrated their efforts on un-dermining Polk's administration as governor, and he lost his next two races for that office.

"Lean Jimmy" Jones, the East Tennessean who opposed Polk both times, could amble across the platform with a snicker and stroke a coon-skin cap just so, and have the back-woods voters roaring with laughter before he opened his mouth. His jibes at the deadly earnest Polk were killing, and "Lean Jimmy" won both races handily.

Polk's family troubles had dogged him almost as inces-

santly as his political enemies and his stomach ache. His father had died soon after Polk went to Congress, and Polk,
with no children of his own, had tried to help his widowed
mother guide the younger brothers and sisters. One brother
had died an alcoholic, and two others died the same year. His
four sisters were married, but one of them was so obstreper-
ous that she kept the family in a turmoil. The Polks were often embroiled in litigation over division of their vast estates.

Polk had taken special interest in the education of his
two youngest brothers at the University of North Carolina.
One of them, Polk's favorite, died of tuberculosis soon after
graduation. The only remaining brother exchanged shots with
another man during a quarrel, killed him, and served a term
in jail.

When Polk lost two tries for the governorship, his glee-
ful opponents said it was all over for him. There was just so
much a sick man could stand.

The Dark Horse
Makes His Play

The fan that Sarah Polk fluttered against her blue velvet gown at the inaugural ball had miniature portraits of all eleven presidents on it—the newest, her husband, James K. Polk. It was Polk's special gift to his wife to commemorate the day she became first lady of the land—one of his few lapses into sentimentality. She carried it to the inauguration ceremonies in the drenching rain that March 4, 1845.

They rushed from the wet procession to the White House for the formal dinner the forty-nine-year-old president and his wife were giving that night. That was the beginning.

Four years later, when the California gold rush sent ships and wagons racing west, some Americans remembered it was President Polk who had acquired that land—from Mexico to Canada, from the Rockies to the Pacific—for the United States. One of their toasts ran: "To George Washington, who did more than any other man to establish our country; to James K. Polk, who did more than any other man to enlarge it."

But in the century between the Gold Rush and the atomic bomb, Polk's fame was almost blotted off the history books. The long silence about Polk's work had come largely because Northern historians mistakenly imagined that the Southern president's motive in expanding the nation was to extend slavery. When the passions of the Civil War had cooled and historians investigated Polk's diary and correspondence, they were astounded at the size of his accomplishments. Polk had in fact devoted much of his energy to averting a Civil War.

Actually Polk would never have had a chance at the presidency if it had not been for the touchy problem of slavery that was muddying political campaigns twenty years before the Civil War.

Martin Van Buren, who had already served one term in the White House (1837-1841), was practically sure of nomination as president, and Polk had hopes of being vice-president. But the big question of the day was whether the United States should admit Texas to the Union, and Van Buren, a New Yorker, opposed that. The "Texas question" was being confused with the slavery question. Northern politicians were arguing that letting Texas into the Union would mean another slave state.

Andrew Jackson, old and frail and less than one year from his grave, summoned Polk from his Columbia home to the Hermitage. He told Polk to make his views known on Texas and win the election for the Democrats. The nation was in a mood to grow. And Polk, even though he had been out of office for three years (defeated in two tries for the governorship after one term), was still a power in national politics. His Columbia home, just down the street from where his parents' home still stands, was bustling with correspondence between him and party leaders in Washington.

Even President Tyler, of the opposition party, offered him the job of secretary of navy during those years of "retirement," but Polk turned it down. He was biding his time for the vice-presidency.

So in May 1844, while the slow-talking, meticulously dressed Polk devised the strategy from his Columbia home, his friends Cave Johnson of Clarksville and Gideon Pillow of Columbia went to the Democratic national convention in Baltimore to work for his nomination for the vice-presidency—and just possibly for the presidency.

The convention turned into a mad four-way contest, with Van Buren leading. It was not until the third day of balloting that Polk's name was proposed for the presidency, and Van Buren withdrew in his favor, throwing the powerful New York delegation to the pro-Texas candidate from Tennessee. On the second balloting after his name was introduced, Polk got the unanimous vote of the convention. All of a sudden the nation had its first "dark horse" candidate, and the opposition delighted in chanting, "*Who* is James K. Polk?"

To balance the ticket, easterner George M. Dallas, a Pennsylvanian whom Sarah Polk later described as "an elegant man, tall, exceedingly handsome, and gentle in manner," was nominated for vice-president. Thus the campaign slogan, "Polk, Dallas and Texas!" streamed across campaign banners, and thus the Texas city of Dallas later received its name.

Polk's race for the presidency was against the famed Kentucky statesman, Henry Clay. Polk lost Tennessee by 113 votes, but won the national election, and that victory hinged on the New York vote.

Word of victory reached him at his Columbia home by fast mail (a Nashville livery stable owner rode all night to get the message there) a day before newspapers received the news. In that interim, Polk took sly pleasure in strolling down his hometown streets as people offered condolences for his "defeat."

Neither imposing in appearance nor endearing in manner, Polk did know how to get things done, and he announced that he would reach his presidential goals in one term. He did—sometimes ruthlessly, sometimes slyly, but always with the conviction that he had to serve the little man, paving the way for the growth of the nation. And the grim man with the fiery eyes shook the country with his new concept of the presidency.

"I intend to be myself President of the United States," the tight-lipped Polk wrote from his Columbia home ten weeks before his inauguration. Incorruptible himself, a demon for work (he took only six weeks' vacation during his four years as president and averaged ten to twelve hours' work a day), he shattered himself in the effort. "No President who performs his duty faithfully and conscientiously can have any leisure," he wrote shortly before he left the White House. "If he entrusts the details and smaller matters to subordinates, constant errors will occur."

Polk made a point of being in Washington two weeks before his inauguration. Methodically he listed the goals he would shoot at in his four years. Methodically, during those four years, he checked off each goal after he had coaxed, brow-beaten, out-maneuvered overwhelming opposition in Congress.

Polk's goals were to: annex Texas; acquire California; settle the dispute with England over Oregon and maintain American rights there; lower the tariff so that it would be just to farmers and manufacturers alike, and thereby put an end to the division between the agricultural South and the industrial North; put an end to financial chaos and bank controversy by creating a sub-treasury, or, as he called it, a Constitutional Treasury.

For years, historians dismissed these tremendous accomplishments by imagining that the going was easy then—that Polk was simply in tune with a Congress and a nation that happened to want to move in the same direction he did.

Actually he was at loggerheads with his Congress, his cabinet, his generals, leading members of his own party as well as the opposition party most of the time. When his four-volume diary, a meticulous record of his White House years, was published in 1910, historians understood for the first time the battles by which Polk steered the presidency into new power and responsibility.

They saw that the earlier estimates of Polk as a pro-slavery president were far from the facts. His drive to stretch the nation to the Pacific had nothing to do with extending slave territory. It was a determined drive to get America's hands firmly on Pacific ports, particularly San Francisco.

He held cabinet meetings every week, encouraged each man to express his views, but was seldom swayed from his own. He had congressmen in to confer with him practically every night. When they balked at his bills, claiming they were carrying out the will of their constituents, Polk reminded them that he had constituents too—the whole country.

Cartoonist labeled him "King James," and his own vice-president despaired over the "cunning that so completely dominated Polk's action that even his most devoted friends could not refrain from complaining to each other, with bitter grief and shame, of his crooked politics." One Whig congressman roared out on the floor of the House that "the whole Government is now virtually in the hands of the President" and a man had either to "stand on the platform with the Executive, or be pushed into the sea."

Polk was the first president since Washington to become in fact and deed commander-in-chief of the armed forces. Cornered into fighting Mexico to win the land settlement he had hoped to gain by negotiation, he had to battle his generals as well as the enemy.

But with all that, he was a master diplomat. When he decided to play his hand behind the scenes in the dickering with Great Britain over division of the Oregon territory (which then stretched all the way to Alaska and had been jointly governed by our country and England), congressional leaders were furious at his silence. His tactics wore down all opposition, and they drew the northern boundary of the United States where he wanted it. At the same time, he thought Britain and France had designs on California, and he wanted to buy it from a reluctant Mexico.

When Mexico finally met his terms, it was for half the amount he had originally planned to offer them: $15 million. Through sheer will and dogged cunning, he had rounded out our share of the continent in monumental proportions. He added to our country not only what is now Texas, California, and Oregon, but also Arizona, Nevada, Utah, New Mexico, Washington, Idaho, and parts of Montana, Wyoming and Colorado.

Polk boiled at the tariff laws that made the "rich richer and the poor poorer," and the legislation dearest to his heart was the bill lowering the tariff. A cold, unsentimental man, he never nursed grudges or cultivated hates. If he found a good man for a job, he appointed him, no matter how bitterly that man had attacked him on former issues.

He was scrupulously careful never to accept a gift of value from anyone while he was in office. When someone else sent him wine, he paid for it. He and Mrs. Polk considered it beneath the dignity of the White House to have dances there, and they cut out that practice. Sarah Polk worried over her husband's poor health, tried to get him out of the White House for a carriage ride occasionally, spared him every possible annoyance, read the newspapers first to mark the stories he would want to read.

"The White House was the abode of pleasure while I was there," she recalled in her forty-two years of widowhood, lived out in Nashville in the white-columned house that Polk bought practically in the shadow of Tennessee's new capitol.

The house had once belonged to Felix Grundy, the canny old lawyer who had first taught Polk law, and the president, barely holding on to his health through his last year in office, must have had some sentiment about the place. He wrote to his mother of his tremendous yearning for Tennessee and years of rest he looked forward to, and Sarah busied herself with selecting drapery and upholstery materials for the new home in Nashville.

Polk battled Congress to his last hour in office, and as he and Sarah stepped on the steamer the next day, bound for Tennessee, he was, at fifty-three, a broken man. His illness was so acute that he had to cancel appearances before crowds waiting to honor him on the journey home, and his arrival in

Nashville was delayed several days because he was suffering from the boat's motion. He could hardly make it through the welcoming ceremonies at the Nashville courthouse square where Governor Neill Brown made the chief speech.

It was spring 1849, and Polk and his wife were eager to start work on the garden of their new home, practically in sight of the state capitol (where a motel stands now, at Seventh Avenue and Union). Sarah was in a dither over the furniture, and Polk insisted on arranging his own books on the library shelves.

That exertion apparently was too much, and it was thought that he fell victim to the cholera epidemic that was infiltrating Nashville at that moment. In spite of all medical aid available, he died twelve days later, on June 15, 1849, just three months after he left the White House.

Polk had commissioned William Strickland, architect of Tennessee's capitol, to design his tomb, and it stood on the grounds of the Polk home until after Mrs. Polk died in 1891.

Polk's will, giving his home and grounds to the state of Tennessee for historic preservation, was broken by greedy relatives after his wife's death. After they sold the place, it was demolished and replaced by a succession of buildings, including Nashville's handsome new public library today.

In 1893, the vault and monument, with Mrs. Polk buried beside her husband, were moved to the "back side" of Capitol Hill, where it is seldom noticed. Not even the men who mow the steep slope on summer days pause to read the tributes inscribed there to the man who "planted the laws of the American Union on the shores of the Pacific."

The Tennessean
and the Czar

A tall, gaunt Tennessean walked the streets of St. Petersburg, Russia, in 1852, watched by eyes he never saw. Police marked every move he made. Secret agents opened his mail. Servants reported every conversation.

For Neill S. Brown, former governor of Tennessee, was United States minister to Russia, and the full weight of Russian intrigue fell heavily on his shivering shoulders.

"Secrecy and mystery characterize everything," Brown reported to our State Department in January 1852. "Nothing is made public that is worth knowing. The position of a minister here is far from pleasant. This government possesses in an exquisite degree the art of worrying a foreign representative, without ever giving him even the consolation of an insult."

Ice-bound in hostile territory, thousands of miles from home and family, Brown suffered so from the brutal cold of Russian winters that his health was almost wrecked. But from 1850 to 1853, he stuck to the post, reporting with uncanny accuracy the course that Russia's scheme for world domination was taking.

"A strange superstition prevails among the Russians that they are destined to conquer the world," Brown wrote from St. Petersburg in January 1852, as the gloomy drama of world ambition unfolded. "The prayers of the priest in the church are mingled with request to hasten and consummate this 'divine mission'."

Brown's amazing grasp of the Russian mind and Russian

politics stands as a model to our ambassadors today. When his own great-grandson, Britains' Lord Hailsham (a leader in the Conservative party today), got his first glimpse of Brown's official reports to the State Department, he was astounded to see how exactly they apply to the Russian scene today. Lord Hailsham responded to quotes from Brown's dispatches:

> I had always been told that my great-grandfather had had some interesting things to say about Russian regime when he was ambassador to St. Petersburg. But I had never seen any part of what he wrote. My great-grandfather's reports raise the most interesting questions of the whole Russian enigma. How far are the characteristics of the Soviet regime which most perplex and exasperate us qualities of Russia, and how far are they the consequences of Communist ideology? The answer is not a simple one. Here you have my great-grandfather writing of the Imperialist Czarist regime more than a hundred years ago in terms which might well have been used by Khrushchev and Bulganin. He [Brown] is appalled by the same hatred of freedom, the same secrecy, the same distrust of strangers, especially from the West. He also notes the same absence of originality in philosophy or moral and artistic ideas.

Nothing puzzled Brown more than the Russian's inability to invent. For long before they imported scientists to devise a Sputnik, they imported American engineers to lay a railroad from Moscow to St. Petersburg. But when it was finished, in 1852, the Russians had no idea how to run it. According to Brown:

> There is great want of skill and experience among the Russians in such business, and many ridiculous incidents occur in their administration of

it. The Russians are proverbial for their powers of imitation, and equally so for their want of invention. Hence they rely on foreign ingenuity, but they copied well. Russia cannot boast of a single invention in mechanics that has been copied or used outside the Empire, or a single book that has become a text in any of the moral or natural sciences. All they have is borrowed, except this miserable climate . . . And all of their arts and pursuits, though cultivated and pressed with commendable diligence and a good degree of success, are the produce of foreign genius—duplicates of inventions and discoveries of people wiser than themselves.

No nation has more need of foreigners, and none is so jealous or ungrateful toward them.

Brown, a Giles County lawyer who in 1847 had become the youngest governor in the history of Tennessee when he was thirty-seven, was only forty years old when he arrived at the world's "most artificial, most extravagant court" to represent the United States. His arrival there was an exotic climax to one of the striking careers in Tennessee history.

His own grandfather, Angus Brown, was a stern Scotsman who came to the United States in 1750 and brought his family up in strict Presbyterian rigor in their North Carolina home. Angus's son, Duncan Brown, moved to Giles County, Tennessee, in 1809, the year he was married, and brought his family up in the same staunch honor-loving, church-loving, book-loving Presbyterian mold.

Most of the learning on Tennessee farms in those days was at home, and Duncan Brown's son, Neill S. Brown, never attended school until he was seventeen years old. Six years later he had graduated from the old Jackson College in Columbia, had studied law and opened his law office in Pulaski.

At twenty-seven, he was a member of the state legislature. At thirty-three, he barely lost the race for Congress. At thirty-seven, he became Tennessee's fourteenth governor, and made valiant fight to enlarge the public school system so that every boy and girl in the state would have a chance to learn. "The chief faculty by which this eminence was attained was his matchless power of addressing crowds of men," a historian of the day wrote.

A leading Whig in the state, Brown was credited with swinging Tennessee for the Whig candidate, Zachary Taylor, in the presidential election of 1848. In May 1850, two months before he died, grateful President Taylor appointed Brown "Envoy Extraordinary and Minister Plenipotentiary" to Russia. Thus, only twenty-three years after he entered school, Brown arrived at the most mysterious court in Europe to present his credentials to the czar.

It was August 18, 1850, and Brown and his secretary, Edward H. Wright, had sailed into the St. Petersburg harbor three weeks before, after a five-week voyage from New York. They got up early that morning to take a steamer fifteen miles up the Neva River to the palace (called Peterhof, because it had been built by Peter the Great 150 years before).

"I embarked on a steamboat and reached Peterhof about 10 ½ A.M.," Brown reported to Daniel Webster, secretary of state at the time. "We were met at the landing by a carriage from the Palace, and escorted to apartments in the vicinity prepared for us."

He had already determined not to bend his knee to any ruler. "In Tennessee, we kneel to no one, unless it is a lady," he had explained to one European. (Though, on one court occasion in St. Petersburg, he did bow so low to the emperor that the duke of Wellington cautioned him: "Don't make a fool of yourself, my boy.")

His head was not turned by the splendor of hundreds of fountains playing along tiers of terraces, or the wide sweep of steps leading from formal gardens where classic statuary was mirrored in reflecting pools; but the spectacle of soldiers drilling, of the clatter and flash of swords seemed significant.

"It was a fete day at the Palace, and the Emperor had a grand review of the Imperial Guard and the other corps stationed in the neighborhood," Brown wrote. "We witnessed the review for more than an hour and were struck with the fine appearance of the troops and the promptness and precision with which they moved."

Having shown off his crack troops ("Display is part of the government policy," Brown wrote), the emperor finally— about 1:00 P.M. —had Brown shown into the velvet-hung rooms where he was to be presented to the royal family: first the empress; then her daughter; then her son, "the Grand Duke Alexander, the heir apparent to the throne," and "lastly I was presented to the Emperor in his office chamber."

Brown was surprised at the "plainness and unostentatious bearing of all the members of the Imperial family . . . in a court so remarkable for ceremony and the observance of all the rules of etiquette."

The introductory conversation was cordial, and Brown was impressed by Czar Nicholas I and his son, Alexander II (who was to be hideously assassinated by Revolutionists' bombs in 1881). "The Emperor is a man of striking superiority, of fine manners and great energy of character," Brown wrote. "His government is moving on with the quietness and regularity of a time-piece."

It was both the mysterious quietness and the ticking of Russia's time-piece that were to torment Brown in the next three years.

He warned Americans that Russians were buying up all the American oak they could find because it was the best in the world for shipbuilding. He warned that Russians considered us the greatest obstacle in their pursuit of power. "Russia occupies and will continue to occupy a commanding position in every struggle against popular rights," he wrote. "And though other governments, its allies and subordinates, may seem to be most active, yet they are but puppets on the stage . . . The motive power is the man behind the scene, the Emperor of Russia. He is the formidable antagonist of the peoples. He is . . . impelled by a hostility to free institutions that admits of no compromise and yields to no relaxation."

From the first, Brown was impressed with the sense of urgency in Russia's effort to get ahead. "No country at the present day is increasing more rapidly in strength and resources than Russia, unless it is our own," Brown observed.

He was astounded at the poor equipment that he had to work with in the American legation in St. Petersburg. "There is no historical map of any kind in the library," he wrote. "There is not even an English dictionary." Plunged suddenly into the most expensive capitol city in Europe, Brown was not allowed enough money from the State Department to pay for even postage, stationery, or subscriptions to the St. Petersburg newpapers. He wrote after a year of cutting corners:

> I regard my style of living as a medium one. It would be difficult to reduce it with respectablility, and difficult to exceed it without bankruptcy. With my family here, my expenses would absorb my whole salary and not be considered extravagant. A man without a fortune is compelled to measure his steps . . . I state that my expenses have been and will be $6,000 per annum.
>
> St. Petersburg is emphatically and in every respect an artificial city—artificially built and artificially sustained. It is dependent for all its supplies on distant regions. The necessities of life are exorbitantly high, while the tastes and habits of the place are extravagant.

Everything "costs more than at either London or Paris." The ermine and jewels at St. Petersburg court set the pace for the city. French was the court language, spoken by all fashionable society, and the newspapers were published in French. Front page stories analyzed symphony concerts, and advertising columns listed English governesses, French tutors, German pianos, English carriages and Swedish resorts. Even high-ranking Russian officials were so hard-pressed to keep up appearances in the lavish court that they stole regularly from public funds, and Brown said that he supposed that no man in the world had a harder job than the emperor.

"If even one half of what is said here of official speculation be true, it is enough to irritate any man to death," Brown wrote in February 1853.

And the emperor's woes were doubled by the great wave of emigrants who left to settle in America, and then wrote home about their new-found freedom. Brown described the Russian attitude:

> Our country is regarded as the grand manufactury of liberal principles, and is more to be dreaded in the end than any other, or all other nations, in this strife between the two elements of power. Those who believe, in the face of all these things, that the United States can long escape difficulties with Europe, have more faith in the future than I have. Our safety, heretofore, was in our own insignificance, our distance, and in the domestic feuds of the old world. That insignificance no longer exists, that distance is annihilated, those domestic feuds are allayed, and an iron rule sways the whole continent.

Shivering in the cold of St. Petersburg winters, Brown saw the masters of propanganda sit silently and sardonically in their ice-caked palaces and pull the strings that made other European monarchs take the stand that Russia dare not take. He saw centuries of preparation for the show-down between Russia and democratic countries coming to a climax. "These difficulties are increased by the fact that the policy of Russia seems not to be based at present, any more than it was at former periods, on settled principles," Brown said. "Expediency is the great test."

There is a "space age" ring to Brown's warnings. "Steam has brought the two continents into close and rapid communication," he wrote in May 1852. "Space is no longer a barrier . . .Our unexampled success tends to rivet upon us . . .the eye of observation . . .Who can tell what *power*, in the pride and plentitude of its strength and resources may attempt?"

In his first winter in St. Petersburg, Brown's health suffered so from the bitter weather that he sent in his resignation, to be effective in May, as soon as the river thawed and boats could leave the harbor. But his health returned in the spring, and he reconsidered his resignation. Instead, he asked for a leave of absence, and his wife and children met him in London to spend the summer of 1851.

During the London holiday, he stayed at the same rooming house where another Tennessean, Randal McGavock of Nashville, had quarters, and McGavock told of the night they went to the theater where Queen Victoria and Prince Albert, along with the rest of the royal family, were to occupy four boxes. "Governor Brown was refused admission because of his colored cravat," McGavock wrote in his diary. "He was very much vexed, of course, but he returned and wore a black cravat."

Brown returned to St. Petersburg that fall to stay until his final resignation in January 1853. He was still ice-bound in May. On June 25, 1853, all packed and ready to sail that afternoon, Brown wrote his thirty-fourth and last official dispatch from Russia to our State Department. He had had his formal "audience of leave" with the emperor two days before, and, significantly, the monarch expressed an interest in Mexico, Central, and South America.

"Then I took my leave of this great sovereign, and after a few further ceremonies at the Palace, closed the occasion of my final audience," Brown wrote. Then, "literally worn out by the climate," and the deceit of a "proud and haughty court," Brown dashed out of the St. Petersburg legation to board the ship for home and thirty-three years more of devoted service to Tennessee.

> With this dispatch and on this date, I close my mission to Russia and shall leave today on the steamer and proceed without delay to the United States. . . . And if I carry nothing else home with me, I shall have at least an offering of renewed fidelity for that government under which it was my good fortune to be born.

Andrew Johnson
and the Hermit

The mystery of Andrew Johnson, the hotel maid's son who was hurtled into the White House in a whirlwind of hate at the end of the Civil War, still baffles historians.

The spectacle of Richard Nixon's being threatened with impeachment in recent years has focused new attention on Johnson, the only president actually subjected to impeachment proceedings. New questions about Johnson, perhaps the most despised of all presidents, appear in newspaper and television discussions. How did he find the courage to withstand the most vicious attack Congress ever inflicted on any president? How did he dare face Congress in a showdown that came within one vote of costing him the presidency?

What had steeled him to become the only senator from the South to remain in the Senate at the beginning of the Civil War? Why had he faced the contempt of fellow Tennesseans, ruling the state with an iron hand while he was military governor during the war? As a boy, what had changed him from a "wild, harum-scarum" youth to a courageous fighter for the Constitution, as he saw it?

Now, for the first time, in a Nashville document never before published, comes a clue to the stubborn devotion of the "illiterate tailor from Tennessee" to the principles of the Constitution and the rights of the "little man."

Mrs. John H. DeWitt, Jr., wife of a Nashville radio and television executive, discovered among her family papers a few years ago the handwritten "chronicle" describing Johnson's early education by a scholarly hermit. Out of that document, written by Mrs. DeWitt's grandfather, suddenly appears the commanding figure of a bookish Englishman—a rebel churchman and editor who fled his country for freedom and became the primary molder of Johnson's political toughness. Like Lyndon Johnson, Andrew Johnson was vice-president when an assassin's bullet killed a president. Pitched into office in the most tragic hour of our history, when the guns of a split nation were barely cool from four years of firing at each other, Andrew Johnson faced the most impossible task ever tackled by any president.

Hated by the South because he had turned on them during the Civil War; hated by the North because he was from the South, Andrew Johnson entered the presidency with his hands tied. Just six weeks before, he had shown up drunk for his own inauguration as vice-president. But on the night President Lincoln died, Johnson plotted the course for the task ahead. He would stick to the Constitution, no matter what.

Johnson's story began in the sort of "out" role that marked much of his life. While a merry Christmas party rang out from Casso's Inn, in Raleigh, North Carolina, on the night of December 29, 1808, the hotel maid, Mary ("Polly") Johnson, gave birth to a boy in the log cabin back of the inn. She and her husband, Jacob Johnson, the jolly porter at the inn, could have hardly imagined that the son they named for Andrew Jackson would some day be president. (Thus one of the three presidents from Tennessee was named for another. Jackson himself did not become president until twenty years after Johnson's birth, but in 1808 Jackson was already widely known as judge and commanding general of the Tennessee militia.) It is possible that Jackson, in his days as U.S. senator and congressman, had stopped at the Raleigh inn, on his way to Washington. Jackson remained the lifelong hero of his namesake, Andrew Johnson, the third Tennessean to reach the White House.

When Johnson was three years old, his father, a popular

man around town, lost his life after jumping into the river to save two of Raleigh's leading citizens from drowning. He died of pneumonia. A monument in the town square later commemorated the heroic act, but Andrew's mother had a grim time trying to earn a living as a weaver. "Polly the Weaver," they called her, even after she remarried.

In 1822 when Andrew was fourteen, his mother signed papers making him and his older brother, William, apprentices to J. J. Selby, Raleigh tailor. According to the contract, Andrew was to work as apprentice for seven years, in return for room and board. A "bound boy," cut off from hope of school or the freedom others boys enjoyed, Andrew was strong-willed, determined. He had his share of escapades, of hunting and fishing, of tearing his clothes on the trees he climbed and drenching them in the creek. "He was a wild, harum-scarum boy with no unhonourable traits, however," the foreman of the tailor shop told a contemporary.

The shop in Raleigh, as in many towns of the premachine age, was a favorite gathering place for citizens. There, as in general stores of a later era, they huddled around the fire to argue politics and hear the latest news. Since many frontiersmen had not had opportunity to learn to read, the town physician or other educated citizens would read the latest newspapers to the crowd. Sometimes as the apprentices bent over needle and thread, educated citizens read from Shakespeare and other classics.

Into that setting one day stepped a tall, gray-eyed Englishman, the Reverend Hugh Wolstenholme, to talk and read to the crowd. One of the most striking men ever to arrive in North Carolina, Wolstenholme was an honor graduate at Cambridge, a former minister in the Church of England, a friend and close associate of poets Sir Walter Scott and James Montgomery. A man of aristocratic birth, descended from five generations of ministers in the Church of England, Wolstenholme was an unyielding rebel.

He had fled Great Britain because he dared defy the king. He had defied the king because he could not bear to see the poor people—the yeomanry—of Britain mistreated. In 1819, when the yeomen in the area of his church in Lancashire revolted against taxation without representation, Wolstenholme helped them organize. When the king's soldiers swept down on the revolting yeomen and killed many of them in the Manchester Massacre, Wolstenholme gave shelter to survivors.

For that, he was thrown into prison for a short time, and stripped of his church. When he became co-editor with James Montgomery of *The Sheffield Iris,* "one of the most radical reform newspapers in England," he wrote an editorial that brought further warning from the government. "That decided him to leave England and come to the United States where the question of taxation without representation had been settled," his nephew wrote in his chronicle. That same year, 1819, the thirty-four-year-old Wolstenholme sailed for the United States, was shipwrecked off the coast of Virginia, and began preaching in an Episcopal church in Norfolk.

Two years later he went to Raleigh. About that time, fourteen-year-old Andrew Johnson became an apprentice, and for the first time heard the fierce teachings of the eloquent Englishman who hammered away at America's obligation to uphold the rights of the "little man."

Wolstenholme's Cambridge accent, his exact and resounding vocabulary, his clean and sonorous voice, his zeal for freedom and learning evidently made a deep mark on the apprentice. A man of "strong convictions, aggressive spirit and fearless utterance," Wolstenholme was horrified at slavery and at the ignorance of the poor whites.

"In the tailor shop of a man named Selby he spent hours each day in reading aloud to the apprentices and to other untaught folk who gathered there for the purpose of listening to him," Wolstenholme's nephew, the Reverend John Hewitt, wrote. The Reverend Hewitt, also an Episcopal minister, des-

cended from eight generations of ministers in the Church of
England, was grandfather of Mrs. DeWitt of Nashville. She
owns the chronicle, "My People of the Mountains," written
by him in 1915.

The Reverend Hewitt, who was 76 years old when he
died in 1920, remembered well his uncle Hugh Wolstenholme, who died at the age 101 in 1886. Wolstenholme told
Hewitt about reading to Johnson on "political and social reform." He fired the imagination of the young tailor with
readings from *The Sheffield Iris,* the *London Quarterly Review,* and other British magazines, plus the political editorials
of James Montgomery and the speeches in Parliament of
prominent British statesmen.

One afternoon when the British firebrand had finished
his reading and left the tailor shop, "one of the apprentices . . . followed Mr. Wolstenholme outside and informed
him that he could neither read nor write, and that the readings in the shop made him wish for the ability to do both.
Thereupon Uncle Hugh made arrangements for this youth,
and any of his friends who would join him, to go to his home
on certain evenings for instruction. This youth was Andrew
Johnson, then one of Selby's apprentices, afterwards president of the United States, and . . . at the time of this occur-
ence Uncle remarked to Selby that it seemed 'a great pity
that a youth of such unusual natural ability should be allowed to grow up in such ignorance.'"

Moreover, Wolstenhome, the one-time minister, took a
more charitable view of Johnson's youthful escapades than
some citizens did.

> At this time, on many accounts, and apparent-
> ly for good reasons, Johnson was practically desti-
> tute of respectable friends in Raleigh, then a small
> town. Nevertheless, Uncle Hugh charitably attribu-
> ted his indiscretions to neglect and ignorance and
> sought opportunity to improve him by inviting him
> to his house for instructions.

Thus Johnson got his first book learning, a preparation for the coaching in reading and writing that his wife gave him later. But it was Wolstenholme's ideas—his insistence on fighting to uphold the principles of the Constitution—that must have played a significant part in shaping Johnson's stubborn will.

Johnson had had less than two years' teaching from Wolstenholme when the sixteen-year-old boy and his freckled-faced brother ran away from Raleigh, breaking their contract with Selby. Notices of their crime were posted. Selby's ad in the Raleigh paper, offering a ten-dollar reward for their return, may have been written in some anger. It described Andrew as "about 5 feet, 4 or 5 inches tall . . . of dark complexion, black hair, eyes and habits."

For two years the two brothers wandered to other towns, making their way at tailoring. But in 1826 when Andrew was eighteen, he decided to return to Raleigh and face the music. "When he returned and found that Selby had moved to another town 20 miles away, Johnson went thither on foot to find him and offer restitution, and Selby exacted money—something of which the youth was not possessed," Hewitt wrote. ". . . Johnson turned to Mr. Wolstenholme who furnished the sum of money and thus secured the youth against the application of the law in such case."

Befriending Andrew Johnson, "an ill-favored youth," did nothing to enhance the popularity of Wolstenholme, who had already infuriated Raleigh society with his "open opposition to slavery, his criticism of those who were careless about the education of the poorer classes of whites."

Added to that came the death of his wife, then his son, then a daughter. Disappointed in the America he had sought out as a promise of new ideas, the rebel minister turned his back on civilization and became a hermit. "Embittered to the point of misanthropy, he betook himself and his gold (from the sale of his British holdings) to the mountains, where he buried himself in a log cabin and his money under rocks and roots of trees nearby," his nephew wrote. "Practically lost to the world for many years and commonly known among the scattered people of the region as 'The Hermit,'" the self-sufficient Englishman seldom had need to dig up a coin to go out into the world for supplies.

But he kept in touch with young Andrew Johnson, who had set up a tailor shop of his own in Greeneville, Tennessee, thirty-five miles away. "When Uncle Hugh needed wearing apparel, he drew upon his gold quarries, walked over to Greeneville and remained there while Johnson made the required garments," Hewitt wrote. "While thus waiting, he spent a good deal of time in Johnson's tailor shop, talking politics, telling Johnson and his political sympathizers how to assert and secure their political rights, and reading to them from the copies of Montgomery's *Sheffield Iris.*"

The picturesque hermit, "straight and strongly built" and "continually spouting poetry," had hoped to spend the rest of his life in the peaceful splendor of the mountain forests, but the Civil War drove him back to civilization, to Asheville, North Carolina, for the rest of his days.

From there he watched with satisfaction the rocketing career of the tailor's apprentice he had fired with his own zeal.

By following Uncle Hugh's advice, Johnson secured his election as alderman in Greeneville. This advice was suggested by what he knew of the methods adopted by the Lancashire yeomanry.

Thus by organizing the laboring classes into companies, by districts, Johnson secured his elections, successively, as alderman, mayor and member of the legislature—all of which led to his election to Congress, to the military governorship of Tennessee, and to the vice-presidency of the United States, from which last, through the death of Mr. Lincoln, he passed to the Presidency.

While Lincoln Lay Dying

The night they came pounding on Andrew Johnson's hotel room door to tell him President Lincoln had been shot haunted him to the day he died.

Oddly enough, in the shock of that Friday night in April 1865, when an assassin's bullet catapulted the Tennessean into the White House, Johnson was thinking of what people would be saying about him today. "I walked the floor all night long, feeling a responsibility greater than I had ever felt before," the stolid little man from Greeneville, Tennessee, recalled in what was probably the last conversation of his life. "More than 100 times (that night) I said to myself: what course must I pursue so that the calm and correct historian will say 100 years from now, 'He pursued the right course'?"

For no man has ever entered the White House with the nation so torn, or with his own role so doomed to turmoil. The country was still numb from the sudden end of the Civil War five days before. Johnson had been vice-president only six weeks. And here he was, awakened from sleep in the middle of the night to be told he was about to become president.

A friend of his, a former governor of Wisconsin who lived in the same hotel, had been at the Ford Theater when Lincoln was shot. It was he who ran the two blocks to the hotel and raced up the steps to the second floor to pound on Johnson's door, and break the news. Stunned, Johnson clung to his friend for a moment. Then he hurried to the little brick house across the street from the theater where Lincoln lay dying. As in the case of President Kennedy's assassination,

Lincoln was shot in the back of the head. Unlike Kennedy, Lincoln lingered on for some eight hours.

"It was evident from the first that Booth's shot would prove fatal," Johnson recalled that eerie night in a conversation with another Tennessean ten years later, shortly before his own death.

The record of that conversation is preserved in a little known document in the manuscript division of the Tennessee State Library and Archives. In it, Johnson's friend tells of his conversation with the ex-president as they sat together on a train on a summer day in 1875. Like a heavy-headed monarch in a Shakespearean play, Johnson recalled the night of Lincoln's assassination.

Alone in his room, he said, he had weighed the issues before him. He, a Southerner, had incurred the wrath of the South by siding with the North during the war. Now he would have to lead the North in making a workable peace with the crushed enemy.

> I knew that I would have to contend against the mad passions of some and the self-aggrandizement of others. Men who had never seen an armed enemy would now cry for blood. The South lay prostrate and helpless and they [the North] would want to kick the dead lion. Mr. Lincoln might have been able to compel obedience to the Constitution and the law, but I doubted my ability to do so. Besides other passions, there was an element of prejudice with which I would have to contend.

By morning, Johnson had set his course.

> Before daylight, I had firmly resolved that constitutional right and law should be respected. The South had laid down their arms and abandoned the contest. The war was simply a big lawsuit before the highest court known to man—that of arms. The South had claimed the right to withdraw, but the

court of arms decided against them, and we had
every reason for believing they would abide in
good faith in the decision.

Thus resolved, Johnson met the delegation of cabinet
members who called at his suite early that morning to notify
him officially that President Lincoln was dead.

At Johnson's request, the swearing-in ceremony was held
in the hotel parlors. At about 11:00 A.M. on that gloomy
Saturday, April 15, 1865, in the presence of most of the cabinet, Chief Justice Salmon P. Chase administered the oath of
office. Andrew Johnson, one-time Tennessee tailor, was now
president.

Ten years later, as he sat on the train winding its way
through East Tennessee hills, Johnson felt the urgency of setting the record straight.

A short, stocky man of sixty-six, black-eyed and firm-
jawed, he seldom smiled. Even in the heat of the crowded July train, he was, as always, immaculate—dressed with a tailor's
pride in detail, one critic had sneered.

On the train he was more relaxed than usual. His old ac-
quantances, W. E. McElwee and Captain Dave Jenkins, on
business in that area, had invited him to sit with them when
he boarded the train at Greeneville. As they sat facing him,
Johnson explained that he was on his way to Elizabethton to
visit his daughter, Mrs. Dan Stover. After settling some family
business there, he said, he would make a trip to Ohio to correct misinformation "made in speeches by Governor Horton
of Indiana."

Johnson felt compelled to make the trip "in the interest
of historical truth," McElwee wrote in his report of that final
conversation. "In fact, Johnson said he felt it to be his duty,
for the time had come to correct many things that prejudice
had continued to utter, which, if left unanswered, would
come to be believed and written into history as truth. He
then began telling about the political troubles that came into

existence at the close of the War between the States, most all of which he attributed to Secretary of War Stanton."

Volumes have been written about the venom that drove Edwin M. Stanton to threaten Lincoln, and to hound Johnson almost out of the White House.

Johnson had known Lincoln since 1847, when they were both poor congressmen, living frugally in boarding houses near the Capitol. They were in opposite parties then—Lincoln was a Whig and Johnson a Democrat—and often voted against each other.

A man without family ties, without school background, without church connection, Johnson struck out belligerently against privilege-seeking of any kind. Invariably, throughout his campaigns—whether for town alderman at twenty, or mayor at twenty-three, or state legislator at twenty-seven, or congressman, or governor, or senator, or vice-president—his fight was for frugality in government and for the rights of the poor man. He leaned on the Constitution to guide and protect American citizens, no matter what their plight. Fiercely aware of the handicap of no schooling, he spent hours in Washington at the Library of Congress. And he made a lifelong fight for public schools.

Where other candidates followed the party line and dazzled the crowds with their oratory, he painstakingly lined up his facts and made his appeal to laboring men, the greatest number of voters, after all.

A swarthy man, with flashing eyes, he had a directness, an earnestness that was convincing. But in the heat of campaign speech-making, his unbridled tongue—sometimes profane and often violent—caused political scars that never healed. A plodder with bull-dog determination, he took the snubs of political opponents and won five terms in the U. S. House of Representatives, beginning in 1853; two terms as senator, beginning once in 1857 and once in 1875; and one term as vice-president, beginning in March 1865, and ending in the White House six weeks later.

In his zeal for the poor man, he advocated policies that would be suspected as Communistic today. He envisioned plans by which poor men would divide the property that had belonged to the rich. He thought there should be no opening prayer at legislative sessions.

He never opposed slavery, because it was an institution protected by the Constitution, and it came under the heading of private property. When the issue hardened into a brutal, explosive wedge, a political tool used to split rival sections of the country, Johnson offered a solution: If Negroes and whites could not live peaceably in the same communtiy, our nation should buy Cuba or some other land where we could deport all Negroes and help them develop their own nation.

Johnson took pride in the work of his hands, in being a "mechanic." Bending over his tailor's bench in his Greeneville shop, he spoke authoritatively of the problems of the "little man." With a reverse kind of snobbery, the tailor rather sneered at lawyers, judges, men of learning who opposed him in political campaigns. He took special satisfaction in the fact that he was still measuring customers for suits while he ran for Congress. (Six assistants helped him run his tailor shop.) •

Frugal, in dead earnest about saving a substantial bank account himself, he took almost pathetic pride in moving his family into progressively nicer homes, until finally they owned one of the handsomest in Greeneville, a two-story brick with acreage enough to keep eight slaves busy caring for it.

A Democrat most of his life, (as a young man he once supported a Whig candidate; when he ran for vice-president, it was on the Union ticket) Johnson was well aware that an East Tennessee Democrat was not the same kind of "critter" that Democrats in Middle and West Tennessee were. The land was different, he said. The crops were different. There was no cotton, little need for slaves in the East. The East's future lay in industry. They were more akin, economically, to Ohio

than to the rest of Tennessee. Johnson actually made attempts at one stage in his career to make a separate state out
of Tennessee and call it Frankland.

But Johnson, in a sense, seceded from the South when
the South seceded from the Union. He was the only senator
from a Southern state to remain in the Senate when war began in 1861. The showdown had come on December 28,
1860, when Southern senators were breathing fire and shouting secession. "Both sides in this contest are wrong," Johnson
told the angry senators on both sides of the aisle.

> The North is wrong in enacting so-called liberty
> bills, in the teeth of the Constitution. What then is
> the issue? It is this and only this: we are mad be
> cause Mr. Lincoln has been elected president and
> we have not got our man! We are for breaking up
> the Union! I say, No, let us show ourselves men,
> and men of courage. Though I fought against Lin
> coln, I love my country; I love the Constitution.
> Let us therefore rally around the altar of our Con
> stitution and swear that it and the Union shall be
> saved . . . Senators, my blood, my existence, I
> would give to save this Union!

The South was outraged at his "treachery." The North
made the most of his courage. *The New York Times* called
him the "greatest man of the age," even as he was burned in
effigy in Nashville.

By June 1861, two months after the war began, tragedy
began to strike Johnson's family. In Greeneville, on a brief
trip from Washington, he was warned to get out of the state
if he wanted to live. He had to leave his sick wife and their
younger children there when he escaped to Washington.

When Nashville fell to the Union army in February 1862,
President Lincoln asked Johnson if he would give up his Senate seat to return to Tennessee as military governor. Lincoln, viewing Tennessee as a key link in the chain of border

states he hoped to win over to the Union, gave Johnson absolute power over the state.

Johnson shouted vengeance at Confederate sympathizers. He imprisoned men who would not swear allegiance to the Union. Mark Cockrill, member of one of Nashville's pioneer families who had won world-wide recognition for the superior wool he produced, had, by his own work, become one of the great landowners and influential men of the area. Johnson bragged to tattered crowds that he would "frighten Cockrill back into the Union by threats of confiscating his land." He threw Cockrill into prison, stripped him of much of his wealth, and said that it would be a good idea to take all his land away from him and divide it among the poor.

Johnson levied taxes on the state, took control of the railroads, and ordered elections. Even as he wiped out the wealth of others, he was shocked to learn that his own wife and children had been ordered out of their Greeneville home by Confederate soldiers sweeping over that area.

The years she and her children spent in Nashville were full of personal sorrow. They arrived here in October 1862, and remained almost two years. During that time, one of their sons, Dr. Charles Johnson, an alcoholic, was thrown from a horse and killed. Their youngest son, Andy, only eight at the time, was suffering from tuberculosis, as was Mrs. Johnson. Another son, Robert, a colonel in the Union army and later secretary to his father in the White House, also drank heavily and later, at thirty-three, committed suicide.

The Johnsons' two daughters, Martha and Mary, were their parents' lifelong delight. Martha had married a lawyer, David T. Patterson, six years before the war, and they lived on a farm near Greeneville. Mary had married Dan Stover, a prosperous Carter County farmer who became a colonel in the Union army.

But during the Union occupation of Nashville, as Confederate armies tried to win back the key transportation center,

Johnson saw little of his family. The capitol building was fortified and known as Ft. Andrew Johnson. Johnson himself, holed up in the cupola where he could watch battle lines form alarmingly near, shouted to the faint-hearted that he would see Nashville burned to the ground before he would surrender it to the Confederates.

"Harsh, stern and thoroughgoing" in crushing all opposition, Johnson won the tremendous respect of Lincoln. "No man has a right to judge Andrew Johnson in any respect," Lincoln said in June 1864, "who has not suffered as much and done as much as he for the nation's sake."

Johnson's courageous stand for the Union so endeared him to Lincoln that the Tennessean became one of the select committee who met often with the president to plan conduct of the war. When Lincoln chose Johnson as his running mate in 1864, Johnson observed wryly: "What will the aristocrats do with a rail-splitter for a president and a tailor for vice-president?"

When Johnson campaigned in Nashville, speaking from the capitol steps on the night of October 24, 1864, a torchlight procession of laborers, "mechanics" and slaves led the way. Shunned and despised by the "best people," he made one of his wildest, bitterest speeches. The old theme of his boyhood—the plight of poor whites like himself—rang like an echo of the preachings he had heard from the firebrand Englishman, the Reverend Hugh Wolstenholme, in the tailor shop years before.

With headquarters in Nashville, Johson traveled widely to make campaign speeches. The Lincoln-Johnson ticket won by a vote of 2,216,067 to 1,808,725.

Exhausted at the close of the hard-fought campaign, Johnson fell ill of a fever and wrote Washington officials to find out if it would be possible for him to be sworn in as vice-president in Nashville. But Lincoln wired Johnson to come to Washington for the inauguration if at all possible. So, on

March 4, 1865, Johnson got in a carriage at his Washington hotel to ride to the capitol with the retiring vice-president, Hannibal Hamlin. Hamlin later testified that Johnson, well known for his fondness for whiskey, had had nothing to drink before he left the hotel. But on the way to the capitol, Johnson became faint and Hamlin produced a flask of brandy to revive him.

By the time Johnson stood before the Senate to be sworn into office, he was in no condition to speak. His maudlin speech, recalling his humble origin, was so thick-tongued and devoid of taste that some senators gathered afterwards to discuss the possibility of asking for his resignation. But one of Johnson's wealthy friends whisked him off to his suburban estate to recover from the fever.

"Don't you bother about Andy Johnson's drinking," Lincoln quieted one of the shocked cabinet members. "He made a bad slip the other day, but I have known Andy a great many years and he ain't no drunkard."

Then in a few weeks Lincoln was dead, and Johnson stood alone—without political power, without tact, with slight chance of healing a country just five days out of the Civil War.

The Web of Hate
Draws Tight

When Abraham Lincoln became the first president to fall to an assassin's bullet, the stage was set for the first impeachment.

The same web of hate that had brought Lincoln's death had trapped cabinet members and congressmen in a furious wrangle with President Andrew Johnson, almost stripping him of office and the nation of constitutional government. The same fury that had torn the nation apart in four years of war spilled over into an unmatched era of political corruption, treachery, vengeance.

In Johnson's private life, there was the steady sorrow of seeing his wife wasting away with tuberculosis. Since Mrs. Johnson was too ill to take part in official duties, their daughter, Mrs. Martha Patterson, acted as official hostess at the White House. Both daughters and their husbands, along with the five grandchildren, lived at the White House during Johnson's entire administration. So did his son Andy, then in school, and his older son, Robert, who acted as the president's secretary.

When the twelve members of the Johnson family moved in, they had the White House completely redecorated and were almost mobbed when they opened the doors for the public to take a look. Daughter Mary installed two cows on the White House grounds, and all the family assured the press they were "just plain folks," making no attempt at society. When they appeared at formal receptions and dinners, the Johnson women invariably wore black—sometimes velvet, sometimes silk, sometimes lace. Johnson stuck to his old rule of frugality, his old habit of accepting no gifts, of giving strict account of government funds. He was aware that his enemies were watching every move.

But at the white-hot moment immediately following Lincoln's death, few noticed the machinations of the evil-eyed secretary of war, Edwin M. Stanton. The duplicity, the plotting, the determination of Stanton to wrest all power from President Johnson reads like a shadowy mystery, embellished with a mad man's fascination with death. For Stanton, who rushed to the dying Lincoln's deathbed to set up "headquarters" for the government in the adjoining room, tried, from that moment, to push Johnson aside.

Stanton, so oddly absorbed in death that he kept his own dead daughter's body in his room for two years and kept dressing and redressing his wife's dead body in her wedding clothes—had, as Lincoln's secretary of war, helped direct the war against the South. But he had warred against Lincoln, too, threatening to split his cabinet and referring to him often as a "gorilla" and an "ape."

Johnson, in a conversation with friends on a train in Tennessee just hours before his own death, was still haunted by rumors that Stanton was indirectly responsible for Lincoln's death ten years earlier. "I made no investigation of the matter," Johnson said. "But it was asserted that Booth had a friend that had been condemned to death (Captain John Yates Beall of Virginia, engaged to marry Martha O'Bryan of Nashville). It was said that John Wilkes Booth had seen Lincoln and had been led to believe the President would commute the sentence, but that Stanton and Secretary of State W. H. Seward had interfered and prevented any clemency. . . . If it was possible to prevent it, Mr. Lincoln could not afford to have discord in his cabinet. It was better to let the sentence be executed than to have any resignations of cabinet members at the time."

At any rate, the Confederate Captain Beall—hero to many in both North and South—was hanged in February 1865, only six weeks before one of his admirers shot Lincoln.

It was against this backdrop that Johnson became president. Stanton, directing the court-martial, saw to it that Lincoln's accused murderers were disgracefully treated, the nation was fanned into a frenzy of vengeance, and evidence was withheld that would have cleared one of the accused, Mrs. Mary Surratt.

The woman whose crime, apparently, consisted of running the boarding house where some of Booth's collaborators lived, was subjected to brutal treatment and a farce of a trial. Moreover, when the court recommended clemency for Mrs. Surratt, the recommendation never reached Johnson.

"The execution of Mrs. Surratt was a crime of passion without justice or reason," Johnson told two Tennessee friends in his final train ride. "She knew no more about the intentions of Booth and his associates than any other person who chanced to know Booth. . . . But her executioners knew the records would condemn them if kept till passion subsided, and they were destroyed."

Even if he had known of the recommendation for clemency, Johnson said, Northern hatred of the South would have made it difficult for him to act on it. "If I had interfered with the execution, it would have been my death and a riot that would have probably ended in war," Johnson recalled the hysterical days.

Historians are still sifting through records of the day to separate fact from propaganda and prejudice. Not until 1900 had passion cooled enough for Johnson to be seen as a man of heroic courage.

One historian, E. L. McKitrick, says the reason North and South made such a bungle of peace was that no Americans had lost a war before. They were unaccustomed to the ceremony of defeat—of complete subservience. Southerners were willing to lay down arms and take up the task of rebuilding, but they were totally unprepared for the program of obliteration that extremists in the North planned for them.

Johnson, who had been violent himself toward the South during the war, defied Congress in its postwar attempt to punish the South. The first violent conflict between Johnson and Congress came over the matter of allowing Southern congressmen to return to Congress after the war. Johnson argued that the South had never left the Union; it had only attempted to do so. Therefore, when they gave up the fight, there was no need to bar any congressmen.

The Radicals, not tasting quite enough revenge, argued that the South had indeed left the Union and must pay a fearsome price for that transgression. Johnson fought those who advocated reducing the South to territorial level so that it could not participate in national government again.

He struck out at those hate-ridden congressmen who thought all white Southerners should be stripped of their property, and that it should be divided among former slaves. Some advocated giving the vote to the former slaves, but not to the white men. Radicals made far-reaching plans for keeping the South so impoverished, so torn by race troubles that it would never provide economic or political competition again. Northern Republicans hoped they could keep the South out of Congress so that Democrats would be in the minority.

There were, of course, moderates among Northern congressmen. Johnson pled with them to work with him toward the moderate course Lincoln had outlined. Johnson saw the Union—the very thing he had staked his life to preserve in war time—crumbling apart in peace time.

He added Alaska to the United States, in face of strong opposition from Congress. He foresaw the value of owning land that reached almost to Russia. Repeatedly he defied Congress, vetoing twenty-one bills, some of them to prevent large corporations from getting illegal control of land. Congress just as defiantly passed the bills over his vetoes. His veto of the civil rights bill set him at dagger's point with the lawmakers.

Johnson still had confidence that he could get his ideas across to the people if he could speak to them directly. He decided to load a special train with top government officials and their wives and set out on a "swing around the circle" to speak on Lincoln's theme of "malice toward none and charity for all."

In Philadelphia, Baltimore, New York, and numerous towns on the way to Chicago and back to Washington, Johnson spoke to enormous cheering crowds. But Northern Radicals had newspapers and pulpits geared to attack him at every turn. "I fought the Southern traitors and whipped them, " Johnson said, "and, God willing and with your help, I intend to fight out the battle with Northern traitors." The Northern press tore his speeches to shreds.

Congress baited him by passing bills calculated to arouse his anger—bills that they knew he would have to veto. When he fired back at them they could accuse him of drunkenness. Enemies in Congress set Stanton to spy on Johnson, and to help circulate the rumor that Johnson had a part in planning Lincoln's murder.

Systematically Congress passed laws that would strip the president and the Supreme Court of power. Congress would rule the nation. The balance of power provided for in the Constitution would be shattered.

When Johnson vetoed the bills, congressmen branded him a tyrant. They watched his every move, desperately hunting an excuse for impeachment. Seven times in the year 1867 alone congressmen tried to begin impeachment proceedings. Bribery, perjury, impersonation of officials were used in the attempt to get evidence against Johnson.

Then in March 1867, Congress passed the Tenure of Office Act (later thrown out as unconstitutional), denying the president the right to dismiss members of his cabinet.

In August 1867, after finding that Stanton had concealed evidence that led to the hanging of Mary Surratt, Johnson dismissed him from his cabinet. That was all Congress needed. Stanton refused to give up his office, and Congress impeached Johnson for breaking the Tenure of Office Act.

On Thursday, March 5, 1868, with all the fanfare of a circus come to town, Congress issued tickets and opened its doors to the great impeachment spectacle.

Johnson himself never appeared before the Senate "court," presided over by Chief Justice Salmon P. Chase—the same man who had sworn him into office three years before. Impatient, chafing because his lawyers advised him not to answer his accusers in person, Johnson remained in the White House while five lawyers presented his case. Most of the cabinet remained loyal.

"The Constitution-breakers are trying the Constitution-defenders," Secretary of Navy Gideon Welles wrote in his diary during the three-month debacle. "The lawbreakers are passing condemnation on the law supporters; the conspirators are sitting in judgment on the man who would not enter into their conspiracy, who was, and is, faithful to his oath, his country, the Union and the Constitution. What a spectacle! And if successful, what a blow to free government! What a commentary on popular intelligence and public virtue!"

Most important of the eleven articles of impeachment were the first and last. The first charged Johnson with dismissing Stanton from office, and the next two involved appointing a successor. Articles four through eight charged Johnson with a "conspiracy" to carry out the first three.

Article nine charged him with giving illegal advice to a general on his staff. Article ten charged the President with making a number of speeches, using rough language and speaking "in a loud voice." Article eleven—the "catch-all article"—summed up Congress's general dissatisfaction with the way Johnson dealt with them.

It would take a two-thirds vote to oust the president. That meant the vote would have to be thirty-six to eighteen against him.

The Radical Republicans were sure of thirty-five votes against Johnson. There were twelve Democrats and six Republicans expected to vote for Johnson. The one Republican they were not sure of was Edmund G. Ross, senator from Kansas who had always fought Johnson. But Ross looked on the impeachment trial as a threat to our form of government.

Vote on the eleventh article came first, and Ross voted for Johnson. That made it thirty-five to nineteen. By that one vote, the Radicals failed to convict Johnson on the charge.

They set the date for the next vote ten days later, and in those ten days the pressure on the seven Republicans who had voted for Johnson was merciless.

At last, on May 26, 1868, the final vote was taken. That was on articles two and three. As the fateful roll call began, the packed Senate room froze with tension.

"Every fan was folded, not a foot moved, not the rustle of a garment, not a whisper was heard," Ross recalled the awful moment. "I almost literally looked down into my open grave. Friendships, position, fortune, everything that makes life desirable to an ambitious man were about to be swept away by the breath of my mouth, perhaps forever." Ross called out "Not guilty!" and President Johnson, by that one vote, remained in office to complete his term. It was the vote, historians say, that saved constitutional government for our nation. No further votes were taken.

Like the other six Republicans who voted for Johnson, Ross had ended his political life. None of them was elected to office again. All were subjected to the hate that hounded Johnson.

After his term as president was over, Johnson was elected to the Senate six years later and took office in March 1875. In the summer of that same year, back at his Greeneville home, he decided to take the train to Elizabethton to see his daughter, Mrs. Dan Stover. It was on that July trip, as the train chugged around the Tennessee hills, that he reminisced with friends W. E. McElwee and Dave Jenkins about what he must tell to set history straight.

"The whole country was in a blazing conflagration when it fell my lot to administer the office of President," he said. "Ambitious politicians were seeking power . . .by fanning sectional hate and waving the bloody shirt. Then too there were many in whose hearts vengeance had assumed the robes of virtue. For them, the South must be made to suffer. The spirit of manhood must be ground out of them. There were a majority in Congress who, like Stanton, were in sympathy with this feeling, and therefore willing to disregard every consitutional limitation. Reason had been dethroned."

Johnson got off the train at Carter's Station, near Elizabethton, and offered a ride to McElwee in the waiting carriage. McElwee, at his hotel, had hardly got to sleep that night when "a horseman dashed up to the hotel and called for Dr. Cameron to go to Mrs. Stover's to see Mr. Johnson, who, he said, had had a stroke of paralysis. I hastily dressed and went with the doctor. Mr. Johnson was speechless and died two days afterward."

When he was buried, Johnson, as he had specified long before, was wrapped in a flag, his head resting on the Constitution for which he had risked all.

The Man Lincoln Let Die

The lock of hair that Miss Martha O'Bryan carried in the locket at her neck to the end of her days was cut from her Confederate fiance's head the day he was hanged as a spy. For that execution of an innocent man, many believe, John Wilkes Booth shot President Lincoln.

There is no document to prove that belief. From the very nature of Captain John Yates Beall's secret activities against Union forces, he had to leave out of his diaries and his letters any references by name to friends and co-workers. Even his betrothed, Martha O'Bryan of Nashville, was referred to as "my friend in Georgia" (where he had visited her), or as "my Tennessee correspondent." Only on the night before he was hanged, when he was distributing letters and pictures to be mailed to family and close friends, did he reveal the name and address of "my sweetheart."

She never did tell anyone that her fiance's sister, Elizabeth Beall, had been engaged to Booth. Martha O'Bryan did not hint that the girl who would have been her sister-in-law lost her own fiance in his attempt to avenge Beall's death. And Martha O'Bryan never thought of turning to another husband, as Elizabeth Beall did after Booth's death.

"Miss Martha," as most of Nashville called her, kept the vigil till her death forty-five years later, dressing as a widow in mourning all of her days, devoting her life to teaching and to the relief of the poor. Born in Franklin, Tennessee, on January 9, 1836, daughter of Dr. L. D. G. O'Bryan and sister of the George O'Bryan who founded a prospering overalls factory, Martha O'Bryan had gone to school to her older sister, Miss Fannie O'Bryan, in both Franklin and Nashville. "Miss Fannie" had begun teaching at Franklin when she was only seventeen, and by the time she was twenty-four she was "lady principal" of the distinguished Dr. C. D. Elliott's academy in Nashville. Martha, nine years younger, came to Nashville to attend the prestigious academy where her sister taught, and when she had graduated, the two sisters opened a day school of their own.

Their school was conducted on the lower floor of their brother's home at the corner of McLemore (Ninth) and Berryhill streets, and the double parlors at the front of the house suited the purpose admirably. When the Civil War came and Nashville fell to Union forces, "Miss Fannie" and "Miss Martha" fled the city, "refugeeing" in Florida and Louisiana with their cousins, General and Mrs. R. W. Williams.

And there the story begins. For Captain Beall, a scholarly Virginia Rebel who had had a lung punctured in battle during the preceding fall, on October 16, 1861, had gone to Florida to recuperate during the winter months, and he met General Williams there. The general, a wealthy man with a plantation at Pascagoule Island, Louisiana, took a fancy to the young Virginian and invited him to his plantation for the long rest he needed to recover.

Thrown together as the general's guests, the poetic, ailing officer and the refugeeing school teacher from Nashville were congenial from the first. Martha O'Bryan celebrated her twenty-sixth birthday on January 9, 1862, and the couple were engaged before the week was over.

Captain Beall, described by a friend as "the most undemonstrative of men, by nature silent, reserved," and Martha O'Bryan, a sweet-faced young lady of great dignity and kindness, spent much of those spring months in Louisiana planning their marriage. To the end of her days she would regret that she did not give in to his pleading to marry immediately and go with him to England where she would be safe with his cousins until the end of the war. From England, he reasoned, he would be able to embark on a Confederate vessel properly fitted out for combat against the Yankees.

But the doctor had warned Captain Beall that his health would not yet permit sea duty, and Martha O'Bryan could not see life in England as the proper course for herself at the time. She stayed on in Louisiana with her cousins and her sister for a time, even after Captain Beall left them in April to rejoin his old regiment in Virginia.

It was a separation to last two years—years when Captain Beall was trapped behind enemy lines and forced to pose as a mill-keeper in Cascade, Iowa, near Dubuque, for a while and finally to take refuge in Canada. Living under various names, he found it difficult either to send or receive mail, but he managed to keep in touch with Martha O'Bryan.

He kept a diary of his activities in and out of Yankee prisons, and she kept a diary of the same period. The diaries, bound in thin black leather and fastened with a leather tab that snapped shut on the front cover, were pocket-size, easy to carry through combat. Out of them came some of the evidence in the trial for his life.

John Yates Beall, descended from one of the great families of Virginia, was born at his father's plantation, Walnut Grove, near what is now Charles Town, West Virginia, on January 1, 1835. His first big adventure was the trip to England when he was fifteen years old, accompanying his beloved grandfather, John Yates, on a sentimental tour of the family estates the latter had known as a boy. On that visit, the young boy suffered a shattering loss: his grandfather fell ill and died. John Yates Beall, alone and heartbroken, returned to the United States.

He studied at the University of Virginia for three years and then decided that business—not law—was for him. Fortunes were being made out West in new railroad companies, and in new land companies. So Beall left the university in June 1855, and he and his older sister, Mary, took a train north, to New York, in August 1855. From there they were to take a train west and join their brother, Hezekiah, who had already settled in Dubuque, Iowa, and had extensive business interests there.

But fate stepped in before John Yates Beall got farther than New York. A message there overtook him and his sister: their father, George Beall, was seriously ill. They returned to their Virginia home immediately, only to see him die a few days later, on August 21, 1855.

That event changed the whole course of John Beall's life. He was the oldest son at home now. His mother was a widow with three daughters and a very young son. John Beall dedicated his life to taking care of his mother, sisters, and young brother, and his thoughts were of them to his last moment.

Beall, who had been indifferent to the piety of his mother and other ancestors to that moment, was so affected by his father's death that a new concern with religion gripped him. He became an earnest student of the Bible, a generous contributor to the little Episcopal church at Charles Town that his grandfather had helped found, and a man so familiar with the prayer book of his faith that it was his strength even to the gallows.

The Beall home, near Charles Town, was only nine miles from Harper's Ferry, dramatic setting for one of the wildest schemes connected with the Civil War: John Brown's raid.

There the Potomac River bursts out of the Blue Ridge Mountains to join the Shenandoah in one of the most spectacular scenes in America. And there Washington established a United States arsenal and armory. It was the crazed scheme of the fanatic John Brown to capture the arsenal and use the ammunition to protect fugitive slaves he proposed to set free.

Brown's mad attack on the Harper's Ferry arsenal on

October 16, 1859, brought on his own capture and eventual trial and hanging at Charles Town. No soul in Jefferson County could escape the horror of what had happened, and military organizations throughout the state sprang up in defense of Virginia.

It is said that John Wilkes Booth was appearing in a play at Charles Town the night John Brown made his fateful raid on Harper's Ferry. Whether that is true or not, it is known that Booth came to Charles Town as a member of one of the several militia companies who were in town for the trial of John Brown. It is reported that Booth gave dramatic readings for the community in a building still standing in Charles Town.

It is also known that the leading families of the community entertained the men from the militia companies when they were off duty. And there are many stories in the Beall family of the hospitality there, when Booth was among the most popular guests.

There is the story that one of the sisters of John Yates Beall met Booth at these gatherings in the big brick home of the Beall family that was center of a huge plantation. Tradition has it that Booth often came there to court Elizabeth Beall (sometimes called "Lily Beall"), and the two were eventually engaged to be married.

But two years after the John Brown raid, war had been declared and John Yates Beall was wounded in another battle. It was on October 16, 1861, near Harper's Ferry, that Beall was wounded in a skirmish with Union forces. As he raised his gun to fire, an enemy shot passed under his right arm, struck him in the right breast and broke three ribs. His right lung was pierced.

That injury changed much of his military career. Doctors ordered him to Florida to recuperate in the winter sun, and it was there, as guests of General Williams in Tallahassee, that he and Martha O'Bryan of Nashville met and decided to marry.

On January 1, 1862, John Beall celebrated his twenty-seventh birthday. The next week, on January 9, Martha O'Bryan celebrated her twenty-sixth birthday. The winter months were filled with debates over whether they should marry then and go to England together. Beall had schemes to raise money for the Confederacy in England, but the doctors had warned him that he was not yet well enough to go on active duty again.

By April 1862, he did return to active duty briefly, but his health failed. He went West then, to Dubuque, Iowa, to visit his brother, and to pose as a farmer and sound out Northerners on their feeling about the war. He found much sympathy for the South throughout the area, and he began laying plans to free Confederates held in Northern prisons.

When his activities aroused suspicion, Beall would cross the border to Canada to confer with Colonel Jacob Thompson, head of Confederate intelligence operations. There were frequent hazardous trips between Canada and Richmond for Beall, and in the latter city in 1863 he conferred with Confederate President Jefferson Davis and the Confederate secretary of navy, S. R. Mallory, on plans to capture a steamer on Lake Erie, made a surprise attack on the Yankee ship guarding the hated Yankee prison on Johnson's Island, and release the tortured Confederate soldiers held there. It was a plan that Beall had worked out during his stay in Canada. The scheme was feasible, Jefferson Davis said, but, since it was to originate from the Canadian shore of Lake Erie, it might endanger the South's neutral relations with England.

Beall had another plan—this one to include bold strategy for capturing Union-owned ships and making them available for the Confederacy. This latter operation was to be carried out on the Potomac River and Chesapeake Bay, and President Davis approved it.

Beall, already discharged from the Confederate army because his wounds had not healed, received a commission in the Confederate navy on March 5, 1863, and he set about organizing a strange party of adventurers, eight or nine men bold enough to seize ships and lighthouses in surprise attacks in the night.

The Confederate government was supposed to furnish arms, uniforms, and some equipment, but Captain Beall's party furnished its own boats and received no pay. As it turned out, they did not receive even that military support they had been promised, and it was only by their own cunning that they captured enemy steamboats, destroyed lighthouses and cut cables.

With two small boats, one black, the other white, christened respectively the *Raven* and the *Swan*, Captain Beall commanded his pint-size fleet from the Swan. In the storms of the equinox, in September 1863, he managed to capture seven Yankee ships and a good number of prisoners and to haul in badly needed supplies for the Confederacy.

By November 1863, Beall was one of the most hunted men in the country, with the Union navy scanning the Atlantic coast for sight of him and his mysteriously effective band of "pirates." But he kept out of sight and scattered his men at the proper moment. By November 10, 1863, he had the *Raven* and the *Swan* at work on the coast of the Accomac, and he captured schooners during the night.

As daylight came and he scattered his forces, Beall remained aboard the newly captured ship and watched part of his small band as it retreated. In one moment of carelessness, his men fell into enemy hands. Immediately five hundred Union men and swarms of small Union boats were covering the bay in pursuit of Beall, but he did not hurry about escaping. He wanted to see what happened to his men.

Suddenly he was surrounded and it was too late to escape. Beall and his men were taken to Fort McHenry, thrown into a dungeon and heavily ironed. For forty-two days, he and his men were manacled, until the word got to Confederate headquarters. In retaliation, the Confederate secretary of navy had a like number of captured federal marines held in irons, and promptly federal authorities released Beall from his humiliation and placed him and his party on the same footing with other prisoners of war.

After six months of imprisonment, Beall was exchanged for federal prisoners and returned to Richmond in May 1864. Promptly Beall went on furlough to Columbus, Georgia, where Martha O'Bryan was visiting relatives. Those two weeks with Martha O'Bryan in the last spring of his life were, he said, "the happiest two weeks of my life."

In the following August, when he was back in Canada again, making plans for carrying out his long cherished scheme for capturing boats on Lake Erie to free men from Johnson's Island, he resumed his diary after a nineteen month silence, and climaxed the entry with the reference to those two blissful weeks.

By Sunday night, September 18, 1864, Beall had some of his Confederate party ready to step on the steamship, the *Philo Parsons*, lying at the wharf at Detroit, and as the boat progressed toward its destination at Sandusky, Ohio, he and his Confederates swelled the party to twenty-one. They all traveled as passengers.

Shortly after four o'clock the next afternoon, Beall had captured the ship, captured and scuttled another, deposited all passengers and the crews on an island. By the second night, he had turned the *Philo Parsons* toward Johnson's Island, where, by prearrangement, a flare was to signal that officers of the Yankee ship Michigan, guarding the prison island, were off-duty on a drunken spree. But the flare did not go off at the appointed time, and some of Beall's men were terrified at the thought of failure in their colossal undertaking. All but three of them mutinied, and in a moonlit scene of unbelief and rage, within sight of the long sought Johnson's Island and the Confederate prisoners languishing there, Beall pled in vain with his men to stick by him until the mission was completed. The heartbroken Beall had to give up all hope, turn the ship into neutral waters and scuttle it.

Less than a month later, hiding out in Toronto, John Beall was at work on another plan to rescue the prisoners from Johnson's Island. "You know I am not one of the giving-up kind," he wrote a friend of the new plans on October 11, 1864. That plan too fell through, and two months later, on December 16, 1864, the police finally caught up with Captain Beall as he waited for a train in the railway station at Niagara, New York.

He and his party were on their way to Canada, about to carry out another anti-Union raid, and Beall was already on the suspension bridge, walking over to the Canadian side, when he realized that the youngest member of the party, a dull-witted seventeen-year-old boy, was missing. Returning to Niagara, Beall found the boy asleep in the station. While he was rousing the boy, the police took over.

From the moment he was recognized, Beall realized the game was up. The boy arrested with him gave away the entire plot when he was questioned by Yankee officers, and Beall was sent to police headquarters in New York City to await trial as a "spy and guerilla."

"I have been satisfied from the beginning what the end would be," Beall told a friend who called on him in his prison cell the night before his execution. "I am perfectly convinced that when tomorrow's sun rises I shall never see it set."

Christmas of 1864, spent in a ground floor cell measuring eight by five feet, furnished with a mattress and a blanket and shut off from a gas-lighted hall by an iron-grilled door, was a bitter contrast to the Christmas of three years before, in Florida with General Williams and the O'Bryan sisters from Tennessee.

On New Year's Eve, 1864, a cold rain fell in the thirty-foot courtyard outside his cell, and Captain Beall meditated on the last night of the year, the last night of his twenty-ninth year. "The year went out in rain-drizzling rain," he wrote in his diary. "Will I see the year 1865 go out? Or will I pass away from this world of sin, shame and suffering?"

Five days later, Captain Beall was removed to a military prison at Fort Lafayette, eight miles from New York, to await his military trial. There was disagreement among lawyers about whether the trial should be held in military court, since federal officers held that Beall was not acting under military authorization, did not hold a Confederate commission, and was therefore only a guerilla. If such were true, then Beall would have been under the jurisdiction of civil courts; yet the Yankee officers claimed the right to sit in judgment. If Captain Beall could produce evidence of his commission and his military authority to carry out the raids, then he could not be hanged as a spy or a guerilla. He did produce his military credentials, from Jefferson Davis himself, but the military tribunal, in double inconsistency, condemned him to death for the very act that would have taken him out of their jurisdiction.

Denied counsel, Beall wrote: "I was doomed before I was tried and nothing tending to prove my innocence was ever allowed." The decision to hang him became official on February 8, Beall learned his fate on February 13, and the next day, Valentine's Day of 1865, he wrote friends and family to give instructions on how to wind up his affairs, what to do with his body.

He was to be hanged on Saturday, February 18, but when the news was published, influential friends from Baltimore, New York, Washington descended on the White House to plead with President Lincoln to reconsider the case. The telegrams and letters and couriers that passed back and forth between the prison cell and the White House day and night did gain a reprieve for Beall on Friday night, the night before his scheduled execution.

Beall himself took no part in it, but his innumerable friends were determined that he should not die without fair trial, and Lincoln listened to a steady stream of delegations pleading in Beall's behalf. Whether John Wilkes Booth was one of the pleaders is not known. But Lincoln did agree to reconsider the case, and it is said that he gave the promise to Booth, then reportedly engaged to Beall's sister.

Beall was at Fort Columbus prison that week, on Governor's Island. The federal officer in charge supplied him with books, including *Enoch Arden*, to supplement reading of the prayer book and the Testament, and he sent his best reading lamp down to the dungeon cell where Beall passed his last days.

Suddenly Lincoln refused to see any more friends of Beall's, sending word that he would change the sentence only on the recommendation of the commanding general. The general, using the same tactics, refused to change the sentence unless he had orders from the president. In that convenient deadlock, the general decided there was nothing more for him to do but set the date for the hanging, and on Tuesday, February 21, he announced that the sentence would be carried out on Friday, February 24.

It was a sort of relief to Captain Beall to have the date set. On Wednesday night, after he heard the final decision, he slept one of the soundest sleeps of his life, he said, and he dreamed of his childhood in Virginia, of searching for eggs in the haystacks with his sister.

All day Thursday he received friends with the poise and charm of a Virginia gentleman in his own parlor, and he sent courteous messages to his considerate jailers, wrote his last messages to his family and betrothed.

But that night, his last night, was tortured by a toothache that he refused to ease by laudanum because he was afraid his use of the painkiller might be misunderstood. The next morning he wrote in his diary of the beautiful sunrise, and he ordered coffee and toast for his friends who came to the cell to share the last hours with him.

"I do not pretend to be indifferent to life," he told one of them. "I had a great deal rather live than die. But if I have to die, I think I can." He asked them to bury his body in New York until the war was over and a proper burial in Virginia was possible, and he asked that his epitaph be: "Died in Defense of His Country."

His diaries, love letters, pictures, and prayer book were to be sent to his sweetheart, he instructed friends. He added, "This will surprise my Mother, for she does not know I am engaged." He called a photographer in to make a picture of him three hours before the execution, and he dressed carefully for the portrait.

As he walked away toward the scaffold at a little past one o'clock Friday afternoon, a black military cape thrown over his shoulders to hang down over the manacles that held his wrists, he apologized to his friends for not being able to shake hands in farewell. And as he stood on the scaffold, looking toward the South even as the adjutant reread the long list of false charges against him, his peaceful mien thrilled even the idly curious. When the provost-marshal asked him whether he had anything to say, he spoke calmly: "I protest against the execution of this sentence. It is a murder. I die in the service and defense of my country. I have nothing more to say."

Before his friends buried the body the next day, one of them "cut from his hair a lock as he had enjoined me to do for his sisters and his betrothed.'" A loose button dropped from his coat as they placed him in the coffin, and that was sent to his mother.

In a burial plot marked by four marble posts and over-looking the Hudson River, the body was buried between three and four o'clock Saturday afternoon, the day after the execution. Arbor vitae was planted around the grave, and there he lay until the war was over and the final burial could be held in his home churchyard in Jefferson County, Virginia.

Whether John Wilkes Booth was trying to settle the score for Beall has not been proved, but many believe Booth was one of the friends at the grave the day after the hanging who swore, "Woe, woe to his Murderer!"

Northern newspapers, as well as Southern, for days published stories of outrage at the lack of a fair trial for Beall. There was much speculation about why Lincoln had gone back on his promise to grant a new hearing. And there were stories about Lincoln's brooding over the hanging in the following weeks.

All evidence pointed toward pressures on Lincoln from the desperate secretary of war, Edwin M. Stanton. New York City had been terrorized by hotel fires set by Confederate sympathizers, and Stanton was determined to use the execution of Beall as an example of the punishment awaiting other Southerners.

Never was there any link between Beall and those who were responsible for the New York fires, but Stanton was pushing for vengeance to bolster morale of Union forces. Stanton made it so dangerous for anyone to be known as a friend of Beall that they had to remain silent. It was as Beall had predicted the day of his death, when he posed for a photograph to be sent to his family and his fiance. He would have liked to have given pictures to several men who had been active in his defense, but he was afraid that mere possession of his photograph would be dangerous. The mere fact that they were acquainted with Beall might get them in trouble.

Then, exactly seven weeks after Beall was hanged, Booth shot President Lincoln as he sat in a box in the Ford Theater in Washington. There are many who believe that Booth, who had toyed with the idea of assassinating Lincoln for months, was spurred to action by the death of Beall.

From that moment, it became doubly dangerous to have known Beall. Family and friends, for their own safety, had to "clam up," as one of them said. Letters vanished. Possible proof of the courtship between Beall's sister and Booth vanished. And that girl, Elizabeth Beall, became a recluse, seeing few people and saying little, even to her relatives, throughout her long life.

President Andrew Johnson, who succeeded Lincoln as president and knew first-hand about Stanton's blind ambition to run the country, even after Lincoln's death, believed that Stanton's revenge on Beall may have been responsible for Booth's revenge on Lincoln.

"I made no investigation of the matter," Johnson said. "But it was asserted that Booth had a friend that had been condemned to death. It was said that John Wilkes Booth had seen Lincoln and had been led to believe the President would commute the sentence, but that Stanton and secretary of state W. H. Seward had interfered and prevented any clemency."

The savagery of the trials of Booth's accomplices—even to hanging Mrs. Surratt, whose only crime was to run the boarding house where some of the men lived—is one of the disgraceful pages in American history. It was too dangerous for anyone who had known Booth or his friends to speak up or to keep any correspondence.

But relatives of Beall in Virginia and West Virginia are

convinced that the assassination of Lincoln grew out of the indignation of Beall's friends over his unjust trial and death. Cheap exploitation of the story by writers for sensational newspapers over the years have discredited the theory for many. Beall's family—outstanding as educators, ministers, government officials through the years—are convinced that there is only one weakness in the story: the written, tangible evidence vanished because it was too dangerous to possess.

"The story cannot, in my opinion, be disproved on the evidence I have seen," one scholarly Beall relative wrote recently. "It could have happened. The one outstanding fact is that every one in both families clammed up and there is nothing but a wall of silence."

Martha O'Bryan visited Beall's family in West Virginia after the war, and she was never without the pearl-rimmed pin that carried a miniature portrait of Beall on one side and the lock of his hair on the other. The pin was buried with her, as she had requested, but the mysterious box that she had also requested to be buried with her was not. Relatives opened the box, decided that the Beall diary and letters were too valuable to history to be buried and left them out. But, mysteriously, those letters too have vanished.

There are many in Nashville today who remember her personal bitterness toward Lincoln the rest of her long life. Never was his name to be mentioned in her presence, whether in church or in school. With her sister, "Miss Fannie," Martha O'Bryan resumed her school teaching in Nashville after the war, and their private school operated in various locations through the years.

Her pupils heard romantic stories of her engagement to the Confederate hero, and once, at least, one of the little girls got a glimpse of the wedding dress tucked away in a big box in the O'Bryan home. But mostly the city knew Miss O'Bryan through her charitable work and her work for First Presbyterian Church. For when she retired from teaching, she devoted full time to those two activities.

Driving a small brown horse hitched to her one-horse surrey, Martha O'Bryan used to travel the city's streets regularly to collect old clothes and food from fellow church members and distribute them to Nashville's needy. She taught women in the poorer parts of the city to sew, cook, and keep house properly. Out of that work and related social services she directed grew a neighborhood center that today directs social, recreational, and health activities for some two thousand children and their parents. Presbyterian churches of the city support the center, and it is named in her honor, the Martha O'Bryan Community Center.

Some measure of her staunch character shows through in a story about her church work to the day she died. She and fellow church women at First Presbyterian Church, in downtown Nashville, for years raised money for the church by cooking and serving hot lunch to business men once a week. Oyster stew was one of the favorite dishes, and Martha O'Bryan supervised the proportions to be sure the men got their money's worth. So, as she lay dying of pneumonia on December 16, 1910, more than forty-five years after Beall's hanging, she may have had her mind on Beall and Booth and the link with Lincoln's assassination, but she spoke of something else to relatives at her bedside. She had one request: she wanted her niece to go downtown to the church luncheon and order oyster stew. "Count the oysters in the stew and then come back and tell me," Miss O'Bryan said. "I want to be sure no one is cheated."

Bibliography

The Big Land Grab

Henderson, Archibald. "Richard Henderson: The Authorship of the Cumberland Compact and the Founding of Nashville." *Tennessee Historical Magazine* (ser. 3) Sept. 1916: 155-172.

———. *The Star of Empire: Phases of the westward movement in the old Southwest.* Durham, N.C.: The Seeman Printery, 1919.

———. "The Founding of Nashville, second of the Transylvania Towns." Henderson, Ky., 1932.

———. "The Revolution in North Carolina in 1775." Chapel Hill, N.C., 1916.

Horn, Stanley F. Interview by author about Richard Henderson's part in founding Nashville. 1962.

Lester, William Stewart. *The Transylvania Colony.* Spencer, Ind.: S.R. Guard & Co., 1935.

Stealey, John Edmund III. "French Lick and the Cumberland Compact." *Tennessee Historical Quarterly* 22: 323-329.

John Ross of the Cherokees

Eaton, Rachel C. *John Ross and the Cherokee Indians.* Dissertation, University of Chicago, 1919. Menasha, Wis.: Banta., 1914

Meserve, John Bartlett. *Chief John Ross.* Chronicles of Oklahoma 13 (1935): 421-37.

John Ross Collection. Collection relating to Cherokees and to John Ross (1775-1866), principle chief of the Cherokees from 1828 to 1866, was purchased from Mrs. Penelope J. Allen of Chattanooga in 1966. Primary materials from 1775-1793 and from 1820-1840. Official papers, including letters, documents, and claims, relate to removal period. Eight "Talks" from Cherokee chiefs. Letters of John Ross (1820-1866) are concerned with matters of state. Tennessee State Library and Archives. Manuscript Division Nashville, Tenn.

Woodward, Grace Steele. "The Cherokee." Norman, Okla.: University of Oklahoma Press, 1963.

Fair Swap or Swindle

Beard, William E. "Joseph McMinn, Tennessee's Fourth Governor." *Tennessee Historical Quarterly* 4 (1945): 154-66.

Garrett, William, ed. "Letters and Papers of Governor Joseph McMinn." *American Historical Magazine* 4 (1899): 319-35; 5 (1900): 49-66.

Goodpasture, Albert V., ed. "McMinn Correspondence on the Subject of Indian Treaties in the Years 1815, 1816 and 1817." *American Historical Magazine* 8 (1903): 377-94.

Horn, Stanley F. Interview by author about portrait of Joseph McMinn he discovered in Philadelphia. Now owned by Tennessee Historical Commission.

Lea, John M. "Indian Treaties of Tennessee." *American Historical Magazine* 6 (1901): 367-80.

Murphey, Edwin M., Jr. "Joseph McMinn: Governor of Tennessee, 1815-1821: The Man and His Times." *Tennessee Historical Magazine* (ser. 2) 1 (1930-31): 3-16.

Royce, Charles C. "The Cherokee Nation of Indians." *Fifth Annual Report of the Bureau of Ethnology to the Secretary of the Smithsonian Institution, 1883-84.* pp. xlii-iv, 129-378.

Winters, George. *The Journals and Indian Paintings of George Winters* (painted 1837-1839). Indianapolis: Indiana Historical Society, 1948.

Punishment on the Unforgiving Frontier

Davidson County Court Records. 1788-1902. Court House, Nashville, Tenn.

He'd Rather Fight Than Crop

Bassett, John Spencer, ed. *Correspondence of Andrew Jackson.* Carnegie Institution of Washington Dept. of Historical Research Publication 371. 7 vols. Washington, D.C.: Carnegie Institution, 1926-35. death, p. 106n.; hair-cutting affair, p. 67, 68, 102-106, 154, 173, 175, 177. Jackson letter to Thomas Jefferson, Aug. 3, 1804; Thomas Butler letter to Jackson, Aug. 4, 1804; Thomas Butler letter to Jackson, Aug. 23, 1804; Jackson letter to Butler, Aug. 25, 1804.

Garrett, William, ed. "The Capture of Aaron Burr." *American Historical Magazine* 1 (1896): 140-53.

Henderson, Archibald. "The Spanish Conspiracy in Tennessee." *Tennessee Historical Magazine* 3 (1917): 229-49.

Jackson, Andrew. Letter to Thomas Jefferson, Aug. 7, 1803. Jefferson Papers, Library of Congress, Washington.

Jefferson, Thomas. Letter to Andrew Jackson. Sept. 19, 1803. Jefferson Papers, Library of Congress. Washington.

Judgment Day on the Frontier

Cave Creek Primitive Baptist Church Records, Roane Co., Tenn., 1829-1865. Nashville: Tennessee State Library and Archives, Manuscript Division.

Jerusalem (later Mt. Cumberland) Cumberland Presbyterian Church Records, McMinn Co., Tenn., 1833-1872. Nashville: Tennessee State Library and Archives, Manuscript Division.

Mars Hill Presbyterian Church Records, Athens, McMinn Co., Tenn., 1832-1851. Nashville: Tennessee State Library and Archives, Manuscript Division.

New Providence Cumberland Presbyterian Church Records. McNairy Co., Tenn. Nashville: Tennessee State Library and Archives, Manuscript Division.

Wilson Creek Primitive Baptist Church Records. Nashville: Tennessee State Library and Archives, Manuscript Division.

Zion Presbyterian Church Records, Maury County, Tenn., 1815-1970. Nashville: Tennessee State Library and Archives, Manuscript Division.

Politics and Pistols on the Frontier

Driver, Carl S. "John Sevier, Pioneer of the Old Southwest." Dissertation, Vanderbilt University, 1929. Chapel Hill, N.C.: University of North Carolina Press, 1932.

Goodpasture, Albert V. "Genesis of Jackson-Sevier Feud." *American Historical Magazine* April, 1900.

Hurja, Emil Edward. Hurja Collection of Jackson papers. Tennessee Historical Society. Nashville: Tennessee State Library and Archives.

Jackson, Andrew. Jackson Papers, Library of Congress, Washington. Also, Nashville: Tennessee State Library and Archives, Manuscript Division.

Parton, James. *Life of Andrew Jackson.* New York: Mason Brothers, 1860.

Sevier, John. Sevier Correspondence. Nashville: Tennessee State Library and Archives, Manuscript Division.

White, Robert H. *Messages of the Governors of Tennessee.* Vol. 1. 1796-1821. Tennessee Historical Society, 1952: 161-187.

William Blount, First Impeachment in the Senate

Blount, William. *Proceedings of the Impeachment of William Blount, a Senator from the State of Tennessee, for High Crimes and Misdemeanors.* Philadelphia, Pa.: J. Gales, 1799.

———. *The Blount Journal, 1790-1796: The Proceedings of Government over the Territory of the United States of America South of the River Ohio, William Blount, Esquire, in His Executive Department as Governor.* Nashville, Tenn.: Tennessee Historical Comission, 1955.

Garrett, William, ed. "Governor Blount's Journal." *American Historical Magazine* 2 (1897).

Wright, Marcus Joseph. *Some Account of the Life and Services of William Blount, an Officer of the Revolutionary Army, Member of the Continental Congress, and of the Convention Which Framed the Constitution of the United States, Also Governor of the Territory South of the Ohio River, and Senator in Congress U.S. 1783-1797. Together with a Full Account of His Impeachment and Trial in Congress, and His Expulsion from the U.S. Senate.* Washington, D.C.: E. J. Gray, 1884.

He Killed Tecumseh

Collins, Lewis. *Historical Sketches of Kentucky.* Biography of R. M. Johnson. Maysville, Ky.; Cincinnati, Ohio: J. A. and J. P. James, 1850.

Johnson, Richard Mentor. Correspondence. Letter to John Bell, 1835, about prospects for being nominated vice-president. Letter to George Washington Campbell, Nashville, Oct. 29, 1814, about inquiry into "causes of the fall of the Capitol of the United States" and to help find out "the part taken by the members of the Cabinet." Nashville: Tennessee State Library and Archives, Manuscript Division.

———. *Authentic Biography, Col. Richard M. Johnson of Kentucky.* New York: Columbia University Press, 1932.

Tuley, Benjamin S. "The Gallant Col. Johnson." *Louisville Advertiser* Sept. 8, 1841.

The White Hot Blaze of Courage
And Then There Were None

Brown, Virginia. Fort Worth, Tex. 1955. Letter about her great-grand-father, James George, and great uncle, William Henry Deardorf, who were among Tennesseans who died at the Alamo. Alamo Records. San Antonio, Tex.: The Library, Daughters of the Republic of Texas at the Alamo.

Crockett, David. *An Account of Colonel Crockett's Tour of the North and Down East, in the Year of Our Lord 1834.* Philadelphia, Pa.: E. L. Carey & A. Hart, 1835.

———. *A Narrative of the Life of David Crockett of the State of Tennessee.* Philadelphia, Pa.: E. L. Carey & A. Hart, 1834.

Curtis, Albert. *Remember the Alamo.* San Antonio, Tex.: Clegg Co. Printers, 1961.

Garrett, William, ed. "Letters of Davy Crockett." *American Historical Magazine* 5 (1900).

Grant, W. W. Letters to John Calvin Goodrich, 1836. Letters from, military commissions for, and claims for back pay by men at the Alamo. Austin, Tex.: State Library of Texas, Archives and Manuscript Division.

Horn, Stanley F. Interview by Author about John Camp Goodrich of Madison and John Hay of Haysboro, who died at the Alamo. Letter from Benjamin Briggs Goodrich to Edmund Goodrich from Washington, Tex., March 15, 1836, about death of another brother, John C. Goodrich, at the Alamo. John C. and Benjamin Goodrich were brothers of James Madison Goodrich (great-grandfather of Stanley F. Horn of Nashville.).

Miller, Thomas Lloyd. "Roll of the Alamo." Texana. Spring, 1964.

Mims, Evelyn Hornsby. "Messenger of Defeat." *The Nashville Tennessean,* Nov. 27, 1855. About Susan Wilkinson Dickinson, the sole Tennessean surviving the Battle of the Alamo.

Williams, Amelia. "A Critical Study of the Siege of the Alamo." *Southwestern Historical Quarterly*, April, 1933.

———. List of 187 men who died at the Alamo. *Southwestern Historical Quarterly*. April, 1934.

Forgotten President
The Dark Horse Makes His Play

Bowers, Claude G. *Making Democracy a Reality.* Memphis, Tenn.: Memphis State College Press, 1954.

Heiss, John P. Papers. Polk letters, 15. Nashville: Tennessee State Library and Archives. Manuscript Division.

McCoy, Charles A. *Polk and the Presidency.* Austin: University of Texas Press, 1960.

Moore, Powell. "James K. Polk and Tennessee Politics, 1839-1841." East Tennessee Historical Society's *Publications* 9 (1937).

———. "James K. Polk: Tennessee Politician." *Journal of Southern History* 17 (1951).

Morell, Martha McBride. *"Young Hickory," the Life and Times of President James K. Polk.* New York: Dutton,1949.

Polk, James Knox. Polk Papers, 1825-1849. Nashville: Tennessee State Library and Archives, Manuscript Division.

———. *Polk: The Diary of a President, 1845-1849, Covering the Mexican War, the Acquisition of Oregon, and the Conquest of California and the Southwest.* ed. Allan Nevins. New York: Longmans, Green. 1929.

Schlesinger, Arthur M., Sr. "Our Presidents, a Rating by 75 Historians." *New York Times magazine,* July 29, 1962.

Sellers, Charles G. *James K. Polk, Jacksonian, 1795-1843.* Princeton: University Press, 1957 (vol. I).

———. "The Early Career of James K. Polk, 1795-1839." Dissertation, University of North Carolina, 1950.

Wallace, Sarah Agnes, ed. "Letters of Mrs.James K. Polk to Her Husband." *Tennessee Historical Quarterly* 11 (1952): 180-91, 282-88.

The Tennessean and the Czar

Baylen, Joseph O. "A Tennessee Politician in Imperial Russia, 1850-1853." *Tennessee Historical Quarterly* 14 (1955).

Brown, Neill S. His dispatches, as Envoy Extraordinary and Minister Plenipotentiary to Russia, from St. Petersburg, Aug. 7, 1850. Dispatches 2 to 34, from Aug. 16, 1850 to June 25, 1853. To Secretary of State Daniel Webster. Library of Congress. On microfilm at Tennessee State Library and Archives, Manuscript Division.

Gower, Herschel and Jack Allen. *Pen and Sword: The Life and Journals of Randal M. McGavock.* Tennessee Historical Commission. Jackson, Tenn: McCowat-Mercer Press, 1960.

Speer, William S. *Sketches of Prominent Tennesseans, Containing Biographies and Records of Many of the Families Who Have Attained Prominence in Tennessee*. Nashville: A. B. Tavel, 1888.
Andrew Johnson and the Hermit
While Lincoln Lay Dying
The Web of Hate Draws Tight
Bowers, Claude G. *The Tragic Era*. Cambridge: Houghton Mifflin Co., 1929.
Clayton, R. and C. R. Hall. *Andrew Johnson, Military Governor of Tennessee*. Princeton: Princeton University Press, 1916.
Cowan, Frank. *Andrew Johnson, Reminisces of His Private Life and Character*. Greenesburgh, Pa.: The Oliver Publishing House, 1894.
Cox, John H. and La Wanda Cox. *Politics, Principle and Prejudice, 1865-1866; Dilemma of Reconstruction America*. New York: Free Press of Glencoe, 1963.
DeWitt, David M. *The Impeachment and Trial of Andrew Johnson, Seventeenth President of the United States; a History*. New York: Macmillan, 1903.
Fleming, W. L. *Documentary History of Reconstruction*. Cleveland, Ohio: The A.H. Clark Co., 1907.
Hewitt, the Rev. John. "My People of the Mountain." 1918. With stories of his great-uncle, the Rev. Hugh Wolstenholme, minister of the Church of England who left England in 1819 and settled in Raleigh, N.C., where he influenced Andrew Johnson and taught him to read. Memoirs in possession of Mrs. Jack DeWitt of Nashville, Tenn.
McElwee, Capt. W. E. "The Mineral Home Rail Road and The Last Political Conversation of Andrew Johnson." Rockwood, Tenn. May 1, 1923. Nashville: Tennessee State Library and Archives, Manuscript Division.
McKitrick, Eric L. *Andrew Johnson and Reconstruction*. Chicago: University of Chicago Press, 1960.
Milton, George F. *The Age of Hate: Andrew Johnson and the Radicals*. New York: Coward-McCann, 1930.
Rood, Henry, ed. "Memoirs of the White House . . . Personal Recollections of Col. W. H. Crook." 1911. Nashville: Tennessee State Library and Archives.
Stryker, Lloyd P. *Andrew Johnson, A Study in Courage*. New York: MacMillan, 1929.
Temple, Oliver P. *Notable Men of Tennessee*. New York: The Cosmopolitan Press, 1912.

Winston, Robert W. *Andrew Johnson, Plebeian and Patriot*. New York: Holt, 1928.

The Man Lincoln Let Die

Beall, John Yates. Diary and Family Letters, 1864-1865. Private collection of Dr. Charles C. Trabue IV. Nashville, Tenn.

Baker, W. W. *Memoirs of Service with John Yates Beall*. ed. Douglas Southall Freeman. The Richmond Press, 1910.

Eppes, Mrs. Susan Bradford. "Through Some Eventful Years." Virginia Historical Society, 1926.

Hollins, Eugene. Interviews by author about Miss Martha O'Bryan, fiancee of Beall. Nashville, Tenn.

Lewis, Lloyd. *Myths after Lincoln*. With introduction by Carl Sandburg. New York: The Press of the Readers Club, 1929, 1941.

Lucas, Daniel B. *Memoir of John Yates Beall*. Montreal: John Lovell, 1865.

Lovell, John. *Memoir of John Yates Beall—His Life, Correspondence, Diary, The Raid on Lake Erie*. Printed by John Lovell, St. Nicholas Street, Montreal, 1865.

Markens, Isaac. *President Lincoln and the Case of John Y. Beall*. Printed for the author, 62 Beaver St., New York. 1911.

McDonald, John Yates. Letters from and interviews with him by author, about his great-uncle, John Yates Beall. 1962.

O'Bryan, Martha, collection. Letters from Martha O'Bryan and her family. In private collection of Eugene Hollins and Dr. Charles C. Trabue IV. Nashville.

Townsend, George Alfred. *Kate of Catoctin*. New York: D. Appleton and Company, 1887.

Wilson, Francis. *John Wilkes Booth: Fact and fiction of Lincoln's Assassination*. Boston and New York: Houghton Mifflin Co., 1929.

Index